D1416743

Title
Deeds

Title Deeds

The hidden stories behind 50 books

Gary Dexter

First published in the United Kingdom in 2010 by:
Old Street Publishing Ltd,
Yowlestone House, Puddington,
Tiverton, Devon EX16 8LN
www.oldstreetpublishing.co.uk

ISBN-13: 978-1-906964-24-5

A CIP catalogue record for this book is available from the British Library.

10 9 8 7 6 5 4 3 2 1

To Isambard

CONTENTS

Foreword

THERE is probably an excellent book to be written on the history of book titles. It would start with the earliest, generic titles of the miracle-play and *commedia dell'arte* traditions, move on to the age of development in Renaissance dramaturgy when works began to be given quirky individual titles (Middleton's *No Wit, No Help Like a Woman's* or Heywood's *If You Know Not Me, You Know Nobody*), take in the arrival of the novel (early novels are usually not called what we think they are – *Robinson Crusoe* is in fact *The Life and Strange Surprising Adventures of Robinson Crusoe of York, Mariner: Who Lived Eight and Twenty Years, All Alone in an Un-inhabited Island on The Coast of America, Near the Mouth of the Great River of Oroonoque; Having Been Cast on Shore by Shipwreck, Wherein All the Men Perished but Himself. With an Account How He was at Last as Strangely Deliver'd By Pyrates. Written by Himself*), and then, fast-forwarding, would discover how by the twentieth century literary titles were in free fall, as in *Preface to a Twenty Volume Suicide Note* (by Leroi Jones) or *Oh Dad, Poor Dad, Mamma's Hung You in the Closet and I'm Feelin' so Sad* (by Arthur Kopit). At this point, an obvious relation between the prolixity of *Oh Dad, Poor Dad* and that of *The Strange Surprising Adventures* would be discovered. And that would be just the beginning. There would be a whole section on title formats, from the spare one-word title (*Perfume*; *Grief*; *Hunger*; *Scum*; *Damage*; *Kangaroo*; *Perelandra*; *We*) to the quotation-as-title (*Brave New World*; *Absalom, Absalom!*; *Of Mice and Men*), to the oxymoronic title (*The Good Terrorist*; *Enduring Passion*) and many, many others. The title-in-translation would be considered (in German, PG Wodehouse's *Heavy Weather* becomes *Sein und Schwein*, or 'Being and Pigs'; in Dutch, EM Forster's *A Passage to India* becomes *De echo van de Marabar* (possibly a better title?); and in English, Sartre's *Huis Clos* becomes, rather indecisively, *No Exit*, *In Camera*, *No Way Out*, *Dead End*, *Sequestered* or *Closed Hearing*). There would be a chapter on title variants (Dickens and Hemingway were two writers who obsessively listed possible titles: Hemingway's lists sometimes amounted to over a hundred) and a lot on the battles between authors, editors and agents for supremacy (*Jaws* was very nearly called *A Stillness in the Water* and *Novel on Yellow Paper* nearly called *Pompey Casmilus*). It would be a good read.

This book, however, is completely different. It is an expansion of a weekly newspaper column called 'Title Deed' for the *Sunday Telegraph*. In the column I tell the stories of how books got their names, and I set myself three conditions: firstly, the title should not be explicable simply by reading the book; secondly, the title should not be a quotation; and thirdly, the title should be title of a book or play rather than a poem or short story. I have stuck to these conditions as far as possible in this book, which is a sequel to an earlier book of essays on similar lines, *Why Not Catch-21?* As in *Why Not Catch-21?* the chapters have been organized chronologically, in this case starting with Dante and ending with Douglas Coupland.

My thanks go to Francis Heaney, for allowing me to reproduce the poem on page 76, and to Michael Prodger, the books editor of the *Sunday Telegraph*, for his support and encouragement over five years of the newspaper column.

Gary Dexter

1

The Divine Comedy (c.1315)
Dante Alighieri

THE Divine Comedy, Dante's journey through three after-worlds, was intended as a puzzle. In a letter to his patron, Dante said:

> It must be understood that the meaning of this work is
> not of one kind only; rather the work may be described
> as 'polysemous', that is, having several meanings; for
> the first meaning is that which is conveyed by the letter,
> and the next is that which is conveyed by what the letter
> signifies; the former of which is called literal, while the
> latter is called allegorical, or mystical.

It was also structurally and numerically complex:

> And the form is twofold – the form of the treatise, and
> the form of the treatment. The form of the treatise is
> threefold, according to the threefold division. The first
> division is that by which the whole work is divided
> into three cantiche; the second, by which each cantica is
> divided into cantos; and the third, whereby each canto
> is divided into rhymed lines. The form or manner of

> treatment is poetic, fictive, descriptive, digressive, and
> figurative; and further it is definitive, analytical, proba-
> tive, refutative, and exemplicative.

As well as these various levels or layers, the story was a fusion of two existing types of popular narrative: the ripping yarn of adventures in the world of the dead (a popular subject since Orpheus and Eurydice), and the love-story (in this case of Dante for Beatrice[1]). It was this incredible richness that made *The Divine Comedy* irresistible to later artists and writers. In English literature, *The Divine Comedy* was there from the beginning, in the work of Chaucer; Milton drew on it, as did later writers such as Robert Browning (who described it as 'the majestic mass/ Leavened as the sea whose fire is mixed with glass'). It was admired by the founders of modernism, TS Eliot, James Joyce and Ezra Pound. It was illustrated by Botticelli, Delacroix, Blake and Gustav Doré, and sculpted by Auguste Rodin (his 'Gates of Hell').

What is perhaps surprising is that this work, so important, so complex, so acclaimed, was originally conceived as a 'low' work. Unlike most serious works of literature or scholarship at the time, it was written in Italian rather than Latin. Dante set out his reasons in the *Convivio*:

> [...] there are many people with excellent minds who, owing to the grievous decay of good custom in the

---

[1] Dante first met Beatrice when he was nine and she about eight. He fell in love with her immediately and later wrote (in the *Vita nuova*) that his heart trembled and a voice said to him: 'Behold a god stronger than I that is come to bear rule over me.' He never knew Beatrice well but worshipped her for the rest of his life. Beatrice married in 1287 and died young in 1290.

world, are not educated in letters: princes, barons and
knights, and many other gentlefolk, not only men but
women, of which men and women alike there are many
of this tongue [i.e. Italian], who can use the vernacular
but have no Latin.

It was written therefore as an urgent attempt to communicate with the common reader, and the title emphasized its 'popular' or 'low' nature. It was originally *The Comedy of Dante Alighieri, Florentine in Birth, Not in Custom*. (Dorothy L Sayers gives it as *The Comedy of Dante Alighieri the Florentine*.) Dante explained:

It must be understood that comedy is derived from
comos, a village, and *oda*, a song; whence comedy is as
it were a 'rustic song'. Now comedy is a certain kind of
poetical narration which differs from all others. It differs,
then, from tragedy in its subject-matter, in that tragedy
at the beginning is admirable and placid, but at the end
or issue is foul and horrible. And tragedy is so called
from *tragos*, a goat, and *oda*; as it were a 'goat-song', that
is to say foul like a goat, as appears from the tragedies
of Seneca. Whereas comedy begins with sundry adverse
conditions, but ends happily, as appears from the comedies of Terence. And for this reason is it the custom of
some writers in their salutation to say by way of greeting: 'A tragic beginning and a comic ending to you!'

The *Comedy* of Dante, then, was not primarily supposed to be funny, as anyone who has read it will be able to testify. The comedy of the *Comedy* was a matter of dramatic trajectory, written for a popular audience who liked happy

endings; it was a 'country song'. It began in the smelli-
est of all possible regions, Hell, where sulphur constantly
assaulted the nose, and progressed to the most ecstatic of
all possible endings, in Paradise with Beatrice.

'Divine', then, sits quite badly with this. Can a 'low', vernacular, accessible 'country song' be 'divine'? And indeed
'Divine' was a later addition to the title. The metamorphosis
from *Comedy* to *Divine Comedy* only took place some time
after Dante's death in 1321. By the mid-fourteenth century
Dante had become known as the '*divina poeta*', or divine
poet. The epithet 'divine' was transferred from his person
to his work at some point afterwards – exactly when is not
known. The first edition that explicitly calls it the *Divina
commedia* was published by the Renaissance scholar and
editor Lodovico Dolce in Venice in 1555. As the biographer
of Dolce, RH Terpening, put it, giving Dolce all the credit:
'Everyone who refers to *The Divine Comedy* rather than
simply *The Comedy* indirectly recognizes the influence of
Dolce's edition of 1555.'

In summary, then, Dante's *Divine Comedy* is not a comedy. And its divinity refers not to its contents, but to its
author. Antique titles tend to deceive.

2

Romeo and Juliet (c.1595)
William Shakespeare

THE idea that love and sex are linked with death, or perhaps even are aspects of one another, is cross-cultural and
cross-historical. Ovid deals with the theme in his *Metamorphoses*, and Sigmund Freud in *Beyond the Pleasure Principle*.
In Japan the idea is embodied in *jōshi*, an aesthetic of eroti-
cized suicide (the current fashion in 2010 is for lovers to
burn charcoal briquettes in a confined space to bring about
carbon monoxide poisoning). Love, these authorities suggest, while not ultimately stronger than death, may be its
equal; and, by embracing death willingly, lovers acquire
human dignity in the face of an inevitable extinction.
Shakespeare came to the theme at the end of a vast tradition stretching back to pre-antiquity, and in *Romeo and Juliet*
he was rehearsing a story that many of his audience would
have known already. Shakespeare did not invent the story
of Romeo and Juliet: in fact, he didn't even invent the title.

The names Romeo and Juliet first crop up in the work of
the Italian writer Luigi da Porto (1485-1529). Da Porto was
a captain in the Venetian cavalry, but after being wounded

in the throat turned to writing. Among his publications was the *Historia novellamente ritrovata di due nobili amanti*, or 'The Story of Two Noble Lovers Discovered Anew' (c.1530). The lovers were Romeo Montecchi and Giulietta Capuleti, and the story was set in Verona 'in the time of Bartolomeo della Scala,' which puts it at some time in the late 1300s. All the elements familiar from Shakespeare are there: the first meeting at a feast, the balcony scene, the secret marriage, the potion that Juliet drinks, the tomb, the deaths of the lovers by misadventure, the reconciliation of the warring families, and characters that correspond with Mercutio, Tybalt, Paris, the Friar, the Nurse and others. Da Porto took much of this detail from earlier works, particularly by Masuccio Salernitano[2], but he was the first to name the protagonists Romeo and Juliet. He was also at pains to present the events as having (possibly) happened. This is not as far-fetched as it might sound, since there were Montecchis and Capuletis engaged in factional conflict in Verona at around the right time: Dante mentions the two families by name in the *Divine Comedy* (c.1315):

> Come, see the Capulets and Montagues,
> The Filippeschi and Monaldi, man
> Who carest for naught![3]

Next to take up the Romeo and Juliet story was a contemporary of Luigi Da Porto, Matteo Bandello (c.1480-1562). His

---

2 Masuccio Salernitano, real name Tommaso dei Guardati (c.1410-c.1480), wrote in his *Il novellino* a series of fifty stories, the thirty-third of which contains several elements of the Romeo and Juliet story, though he calls them Mariotto and Giannozza.

3 Canto VI of the *Purgatorio*.

hugely influential series of *Novelle* (1554) included the story of Giulietta and Romeo, and the tale was translated into several European languages, including French and English. (In fact in the mid-fifteenth century Romeo and Juliet were enjoying a vogue – the story was also dealt with by a poetess, the euphoniously-named Clitia, an inhabitant of Verona, who published a poem in *ottava rima* by the title of '*L'infelice amore dei due fedelissimi amanti Giulia e Romeo*' in 1553.) Bandello's English translator was William Painter, whose best-seller *The Palace of Pleasure* (1566-7) included 'The Goodly Hystory of the True and Constant Love of Rhomeo and Julietta' (1567). It is to Painter that we owe many of the plots of Renaissance drama, including *All's Well That Ends Well*, *Timon of Athens* and *The Duchess of Malfi*, as well as works by Beaumont and Fletcher, Massinger, Marston and many others, all of which have Italian themes: if you've ever wondered why Elizabethan drama is so obsessed with bloody and foul doings at foreign courts, it is largely Painter who is to blame.

But although Bandello, Painter and other European translators and adapters had all been there before Shakespeare, one further treatment of the Romeo and Juliet story provided his main source. This was the poem *The Tragicall Historye of Romeus and Juliet, containing a rare Example of true Constancie: with the subtill Counsels, and Practices of an old Fryer, and their ill event* (1562) by Arthur Brooke. Not much is known about Brooke except that he drowned the year after publishing his poem, but intriguingly, he mentions in his introduction that he has recently seen a play of *Romeo and Juliet*, one that was received 'with commendation'. If this is true, then it is quite conceivable that Shakespeare knew of it too.[4] In any case, Shakespeare certainly had Brooke's poem at hand as he wrote his play, since the two works share elements that no two other texts share. In Brooke's poem, for example, it is Friar John who carries Romeo's letter, not 'Anselme', as in Painter; both Brooke and Shakespeare call the residence of the Capulets 'Freetown', a detail found in no other source; and in many other instances Shakespeare builds his verse on hints found in Brooke but nowhere else.

Shakespeare's titles reveal a good deal of his borrowings. *King Lear* existed previously as *King Leir* (in Holinshed's *Chronicles* but also as an anonymous play of c.1590); *Hamlet* was 'Amleth' in the *Gesta Danorum* of Saxo Grammaticus; *Cymbeline* was 'Kymbeline' in Holinshed; *Othello* was 'Othuel', a Moor of French medieval romance; and Timon of Athens was previously *Timon the Misanthrope* by the Greek satirist Lucian (as well as deriving from Painter). TS Eliot, talking about Jacobean drama, said: 'Immature poets imitate: mature poets steal.' For Shakespeare there would have been little distinction. Both imitation and theft were part of the playwright's toolbox, and Shakespeare, one hand on his Painter, the other trailing in the lazy waters of Brooke, used and reworked an entire European literature for his purposes. He changed barely any element of the Romeo and Juliet story as it had come down to him, merely altering the telling of it – which, of course, was everything.

---

4 The situation is rather analogous to the situation with *Hamlet*, in which scholars concede that there was a very probably a lost *ur-Hamlet* which Shakespeare drew upon (and perhaps even wrote himself); in the same way there may also have been an *ur-Romeo and Juliet*.

3

Cadenus and Vanessa (1713)
Jonathan Swift

WHAT do the names 'Pamela' and 'Vanessa' have in common? Apart from having three syllables and ending in 'a'? The answer is that neither name existed until it was invented by a poet. Sir Philip Sidney invented 'Pamela' (see chapter 5) and Jonathan Swift invented 'Vanessa'.

To re-name someone is a peculiarly intimate act, not without a suggestion of possessive control. Ladies re-name their maids, sailors re-name captured vessels, and lovers re-name their loves. Re-naming seems to have been the first order of the day for Swift whenever he became particularly close to a woman: Jane Waring, an early attachment, he styled 'Varina'; Esther Johnson, perhaps the most important woman in his life and the addressee of his journal, became 'Stella'; and Esther Vanhomrigh, the most ill-starred of the three, became 'Vanessa'.

Esther Vanhomrigh was born on February 14 1690, the daughter of Bartholomew Vanhomrigh, a Dublin merchant. Her father died in 1703, leaving enough money for Esther to enter London society. In 1708, while in London on political business, Swift was introduced to the eighteen-year-old Esther, as well as to her mother and sister Mary. He took to the family immediately, and began to spend more and more time at the Vanhomrighs, using as excuse that he kept his best periwig there: by 1711 his visits were so frequent that he had to defend his behaviour to Stella, saying: 'You say they are of no consequence; why, they keep as good female company as I do male; I see all the drabs of quality at this end of the town with them.' Swift became Esther's tutor, and gave her the pet-name 'Vanessa'. The name derived from the 'Van' of 'Vanhomrigh' plus the first part of 'Esther' (she was known among her family as 'Essy' or 'Essa').

Without Swift's intervention the name Vanessa would never have existed. There would have been no Vanessa Bell, no Vanessa Redgrave, no Vanessa Paradis and no Vanessa-Mae.

As for Esther Vanhomrigh herself, intoxicated by Swift's learning, charm and status (he was by this time moving in the inner circles of the Whig government as a representative of the Irish Church), she fell in love. Naturally Swift was flattered, perhaps returned her affections and perhaps began a sexual relationship with her. By 1714, however, he felt things were running out of control (he already had one mistress, Stella) and fled back to Ireland. This did not solve matters. Vanessa followed him, taking up residence at Celbridge, outside Dublin. Perhaps to placate her, the previous year Swift had written the long poem *Cadenus and Vanessa*, probably composed in 1713 and published as a book in 1726. 'Cadenus' was in reference to Swift himself, since by shuffling the letters around, you get 'Decanus', the Latin for 'Dean', and Swift had been made a dean in that year.

The poem – among other things – charts the progress of their affair. Swift describes the transformation from pupil to lover via the arrow of Cupid ('the boy'):

> Cadenus many things had writ:
> Vanessa much esteem'd his wit,
> And call'd for his poetic works:
> Meantime the boy in secret lurks;
> And, while the book was in her hand,
> The urchin from his private stand
> Took aim, and shot with all his strength
> A dart of such prodigious length,
> It pierced the feeble volume through,
> And deep transfixed her bosom too.

The result was not without aspects of the absurd, given the disparity in their ages:

> Vanessa, not in years a score,
> Dreams of a gown of forty-four;
> Imaginary charms can find
> In eyes with reading almost blind:
> Cadenus now no more appears
> Declined in health, advanced in years.
> She fancies music in his tongue;
> Nor farther looks, but thinks him young.

Vanessa herself speaks, explaining what has led her to this pass:

> I knew, by what you said and writ,
> How dangerous things were men of wit;
> You caution'd me against their charms,
> But never gave me equal arms;
> Your lessons found the weakest part,
> Aim'd at the head, but reach'd the heart.

At the poem's conclusion, with disappointing self-censorship, Swift draws a veil over the outcome of the affair[5]:

> But what success Vanessa met
> Is to the world a secret yet.
> Whether the nymph, to please her swain,
> Talks in a high romantic strain;
> Or whether he at last descends
> To acte with less seraphic ends;
> Or to compound the business, whether
> They temper love and books together;
> Must never to mankind be told,
> Nor shall the conscious Muse unfold.

Fortunately we have Vanessa's letters to the Dean to fill in the gaps; and these show that, whether or not the relationship was a sexual one, Vanessa was well and truly smitten. In 1714 she wrote:

---

5 Whether they had a sexual relationship turns, oddly, on the interpretation in Swift's letters of the word 'coffee'. Horace Walpole wrote to a friend that 'There is one [letter] to his Miss Vanhomrigh, from which I think it plain he lay with her, notwithstanding his supposed incapacity, yet not doing much honour to that capacity, for he says he can drink coffee but once a week, and I think you will see very clearly what he means by coffee.' And indeed Swift does seem to play very heavily on the word, among other instances writing to Vanessa on July 5 1721: 'I have drank no coffee since I left you, nor intend till I see you again: there is none worth drinking but yours, if myself may be the judge.'

Tis impossible to describe what I have suffered since I saw you last; I am sure I could have born the rack much better than those killing, killing words of yours. Sometimes I have resolved to die without seeing you more, but those resolves, to your misfortune, did not last long: for there is something in human nature that prompts one so to find relief in this world, I must give way to it, and beg you'd see me, and speak kindly to me, for I am sure you would not condemn any one to suffer what I have done, could you but know it.

She is still utterly under Swift's spell in 1720, writing:

Put my passion under the utmost restraint, send me as distant from you as the earth will allow, yet you cannot banish those charming ideas which will ever stick by me whilst I have the use of memory. Nor is the love I bear you only seated in my soul; for there is not a single atom of my frame that is not blended with it. Therefore, don't flatter yourself that separation will ever change my sentiments; for I find myself unquiet in the midst of silence, and my heart is at once pierced with sorrow and love. For Heaven's sake, tell me what has caused this prodigious change on you, which I have found of late. If you have the least remains of pity for me left, tell me tenderly: No; don't tell it, so that it may cause my present death, and don't suffer me to live a life like a languishing death, which is the only life I can lead, if you have lost any of your tenderness for me.

Swift was in a quandary: he could not marry Vanessa without hurting Stella, or Stella without crushing Vanessa, and so kept them both unmarried and dependent on him. Finally Vanessa could endure no more, and, according to early biographers, wrote to Stella demanding that she make plain the nature of her relationship with Swift. Stella forwarded the letter to Swift, and Swift rode to Celbridge where he flung the letter on the ground in front of Vanessa, riding off again without a word. Vanessa died a few weeks later, Samuel Johnson thought of a broken heart: 'She thought herself neglected, and died of disappointment; having ordered by her will the poem to be published, in which Cadenus had proclaimed her excellence, and confessed his love.'

Such is the unravelling of *Cadenus and Vanessa*, a title uniquely composed of two neologisms; or, more accurately, an anagram and a neonym. In later years Swift consistently denigrated the poem, saying that it was 'only a cavalier business' and 'a trifle'. And there was one other person in whose interests it was to agree. Samuel Johnson relates an anecdote in which Stella was present when two gentlemen were discussing the poem:

> [I]t happened one day that some gentlemen dropt in to dinner, who were strangers to Stella's situation; and as the poem of 'Cadenus and Vanessa' was then the general topic of conversation, one of them said, 'Surely that Vanessa must be an extraordinary woman, that could inspire the Dean to write so finely upon her.' Mrs. Johnson smiled, and answered, 'that she thought that point not quite so clear; for it was well known the Dean could write finely upon a broomstick.'

4

The Dunciad (1728)
Alexander Pope

THE *Dunciad* is Pope's famous exercise in sustained
viciousness. Its main target, in the original version of 1728,
was Lewis Theobald, the author of *Shakespeare Restored*[6],
who had criticized Pope's edition of Shakespeare; but
it also made attacks on other 'dunces' and on the Whig
political establishment generally. Pope envisioned a uni-
verse ruled by the goddess Dulness, who at the end of the
poem overwhelms all literary and indeed human effort:

> Philosophy, that touch'd the heavens before,
> Shrinks to her hidden cause and is no more:
> See Physic beg the Stagirite's defence!
> See Metaphysic call for aid on Sense!
> See Mystery to Mathematics fly!
> In vain they gaze, turn giddy, rave, and die.
> Thy hand, great Dulness! lets the curtain fall,
> And universal Darkness buries all.

---

6 Theobald, or Tibbald, was the critic who maintained that *Double Falsehood* was a Shakespeare collaboration, an opinion only finally accepted by the Arden Shakespeare in March
2010. Pope sneered particularly at this attribution. In later editions Theobald was replaced
by Colley Cibber, the poet laureate.

The Dunciad brought Pope what one suspects he secretly wanted: immense controversy accompanied by physical threats. When he went out of the house he found it prudent to carry loaded pistols, and take along his Great Dane, Bounce, who must have stood almost as high at the shoulder as he did.[7]

Pope's working title for *The Dunciad* was 'The Progress of Dulness' or 'The Poem of Dulness'. In January 1728 he wrote to Swift:

> It grieves me to the soul that I cannot send you my chef-
> d'oeuvre, the poem of Dulness, which, after I am dead
> and gone, will be printed with a large commentary, and
> lettered on the back, Pope's Dulness. I send you, however,
> what most nearly relates to yourself, the inscription to it.

In March, Pope, evidently deciding that 'Pope's Dulness' would give too much ammunition to his critics, changed his mind, writing to Swift of:

> My Dulness (which, by the way, for the future you are to
> call by a more pompous name, the Dunciad).

In the prologue to the first edition, 'The Publisher to the Reader', Pope expanded on his choice of title with mock-serious scholarship:

> Hence also we learn the true Title of the Poem; which,
> with the same certainty as we call that of Homer the

---

7 Pope was around 4ft tall.

Iliad, of Virgil the Aeneid, of Camoens the Lusiad, of
Voltaire the Henriad, we may pronounce could have
been, and can be, no other, than The Dunciad.

In the prologue to *The Dunciad Variorum* of 1729 he went
further – as far as only the truly daring might go – claiming
that the first *Dunciad* had actually been *written* by Homer:

> And thus it doth appear, that the first Dunciad was the
> first Epic poem, written by *Homer* himself, and anterior
> even to the Iliad or Odyssey.
>
> Now forasmuch as our Poet had translated those
> two famous works of *Homer* which are yet left; he did
> conceive it in some sort his duty to imitate that also
> which was lost: And was therefore induced to bestow on
> it the same Form which *Homer's* is reported to have had,
> namely that of Epic poem, with a title also framed after
> the antient *Greek* manner, to wit, that of *Dunciad*.

The Dunciad was published on Saturday May 18, 1728, and
threw London into uproar. This is probably not the place to
go into the various wars of *The Dunciad* – into the accounts by
Colley Cibber of Pope's visit to a brothel, and Pope's demo-
lition for all time of Cibber – except to say that the titular
aspect of the situation was to the fore. One of the first pieces
published in reaction was by a Whig-supporting publisher,
Edmund Curll, who brought out a *Popiad* later that same
year. *The Female Dunciad*, also of 1728, satirized Pope, meta-
morphosing him into a stinging-nettle. Other early responses
were the *Dulcinead* (1729), *Martiniad* (1729) and *Tamiad* (1733).
There were two *Scribleriad*s, of 1742 and 1751.

Soon the various -ads grew entirely divorced from happenings in and around the Twickenham grotto. Satirists produced *Thespiads*, *Rosciads*, *Censoriads*, *Baviads*, *Maeviads*, *Druriads* and *Dorriads*. There were epic poems in praise or damnation of a particular activity, such as the *Golfiad*, *Chessiad* or *Ballooniad*; one early piece was the *Beeriad*, of 1736, 'An Heroic Poem, in Two Cantos, the first being an imitation of The Dunciad, the second a description of a Ram Feast, held annually in a particular small district of Hampshire,' which opened in imitation of the *Aeneid*:

> Beer and the men (a mighty theme!) I sing,
> Who to their mouths the brimming Pitcher bring.
> Say Sons of midnight! (since yourselves inspire,
> This drunken Work; so Jove and Drink require!)
> Say from what cause, in vain unquench'd the Thirst,
> Still reigns to-day as potent as at first.

There were -ads of particular places, such as the *Indiad*, *Hiberniad*, *Helvetiad*, and with marvellous bathos, *Sudburiad*; or of particular persons, such as the *Pittiad*, *Hamiltoniad*, and (most ridiculously) the *Sarah-ad*, in reference to the Duchess of Marlborough. Nor was the animal kingdom neglected. The *Lousiad* of 1786 by Peter Pindar (pseudonym of John Wolcot) was based on an incident in the home-life of George III. When the king found a louse on his dinner plate, he ordered his kitchen staff to be shaved:

The Louse I sing, who, from some head unknown,
Yet born and educated near a throne,
Dropped down (so willed the dread decree of fate!)
With legs wide sprawling on the monarch's plate:
Far from the raptures of a wife's embrace,
Far from the gambols of a tender race,
Whose little feet he taught with care to tread
Amidst the wide dominions of the head;
Led them to daily food with fond delight,
And taught the tiny wanderers where to bite;
To hide, to run, advance, or turn their tails,
When hostile combs attacked, or vengeful nails:
Far from those pleasing scenes ordained to roam,
Like wise Ulysses, from his native home;
Yet like that sage, though forced to roam and mourn,
Like him, alas, not fated to return!

In the 1880s the genre was still going strong. The *Electriad* of c.1885 presented a pantheon of ageing and infirm gods:

Within his tent Achilles sat and swore;
With pain the hero's face was sicklied o'er,
Gout in his feet, neuralgia in his jaws,
Too weak, alas, to fight for Grecian cause;
Bronchitis, rheumatism, lungs and liver,
Hurried him fast towards the Stygian river.

In the period from 1728 to around 1900 there were also, in alphabetical order, a *Billiad, Blueviad, Burniad, Christiad, Columbiad, Consuliad, Dapiad, Diaboliad, Euterpeiad, Fijiad, Fribbleriad, Hilliad, Jeffersoniad, Keppeliad, Lentiad, Macaroniad, Mobiad, Moneiad, Obliviad, Olympiad, Porcupiniad,*

Prussiad, Puffiad, Rodiad[8], *Rolliad, Siddoniad, Toriad, Tauroboliad, Triad* and *Victoriad* – by no means an exhaustive list. It was perhaps the most widespread titling strategy of the late eighteenth and nineteenth centuries. Some were prose satires, some poetic; some were a few lines long, others many thousands. One of 1874 perhaps sums up the genre, and echoes Homer's original most effectively: it was the political satire *The Siliad*, by Grenville Murray.

All of these titles were dependent crucially on Alexander Pope, who had established for all time that if you wanted to make a satirical point, an *-ad* was the only thing to add.

---

8 A poem of 1813 by George Coleman in praise of flagellation: 'Delightful Sport! whose never failing charm / Makes young blood tingle, and keeps old blood warm.'

5

Pamela, or Virtue Rewarded (1740)
Samuel Richardson

SOME books become so popular that their titles enter the language. *Utopia* and *Catch-22* are examples: *Pamela* is another. Before its publication, there were no Pamelas, or almost none.

Pamela in 1740 engendered a sort of mania. A modern parallel might be the JK Rowling phenomenon, except for the fact that *Pamela* additionally contained large doses of sex. The plot concerns a serving-maid, the 15-year-old Pamela, whose master, the wealthy Mr B., repeatedly attempts to seduce her. She in turn repeatedly thwarts him, sometimes by the conventional means of pleading, struggling, weeping and fleeing, sometimes by going into epileptic fits, ratcheting up the narrative/erotic tension to frankly unbearable levels. At last Mr B. is forced to propose, and she weds him. This is the meaning of the subtitle *Virtue Rewarded*: Pamela possesses a commodity, virginity, that can be bargained up to and including the point of marriage.

Richardson said on the title page that it was written 'in order to cultivate the Principles of Virtue and Religion in the Minds of the Youth of Both Sexes' – and that it was done 'without raising a single idea throughout the Whole, that shall shock the exactest Purity, even in those tender Instances where the exactest Purity would be most apprehensive' – which was nonsense. There are numerous highly inflammatory scenes in *Pamela*, such as when Mr B. hides in a wardrobe to spy on Pamela undressing, or surprises her by thrusting his 'Hand into [her] Bosom'. A modern critic, Ian Watt, called *Pamela* 'a mixture of sermon and striptease,' and mid-eighteenth-century England was ripe for it. The *Pamela* phenomenon was perhaps the world's first multimedia event: there were *Pamela* waxworks, *Pamela* fans, exhibitions of paintings based on the life of Pamela, *Pamela* stage-plays (one acted in by the young David Garrick), and a *Pamela* opera. It spawned an industry of imitators and commentators. A genre of novels known as 'Anti-Pamelas' emerged to counter the idea of Pamela as a sweet and virtuous naïf, presenting her instead as a calculating harlot. The first of these was Henry Fielding's *Shamela*[9] of 1741, closely followed by Elizabeth Haywood's *Anti-Pamela, or Feign'd Innocence Detected* and James Parry's *The True Anti-Pamela, or the Memoirs of Mr James Parry* (both 1741). In *Pamela Censured* (also 1741), Charles Batten asked:

> Pamela under the Notion of being a Virtuous modest
> Girl will be introduced into all Families, and when she
> gets there, what Scenes does she represent? Why a fine

---

9 *Shamela* was Fielding's first novel. His second novel, *Joseph Andrews*, was about the 'brother' of Pamela.

Gentleman endeavoring to debauch a beautiful Girl of
Sixteen.

Sermons on *Pamela* were delivered in churches, and the
craze spread to the continent, where in Italy there were
plays called *Pamela Nubile* and *Pamela Maritata*. The world
was divided into Pamelists and Antipamelists, and probably still is today.

Although the name Pamela was very unusual in 1740,
Richardson did not invent it. That honour goes to Sir Philip
Sidney, the Elizabethan knight now known chiefly for giving his last drop of water to a fellow soldier. Sidney was
the author of *Arcadia*, a prose romance written around 1580
for his sister the Countess of Pembroke. It is in *Arcadia* that
the name 'Pamela' first appears in any written text, and it
is very likely that Sidney, an inveterate coiner of names,
invented it, cobbling it together from the Greek *pan* and
meli, meaning 'all honey'.

Richardson knew *Arcadia* well. Before the phenomenal
success of *Pamela*, he earned his living as a printer, and
had reprinted Sidney's collected works, including *Arcadia*,
in 1724-5. Reading *Arcadia*, it becomes clear that Richardson lifted the name Pamela for a reason. The two Pamelas
are strikingly alike. Both are beautiful, spirited young
women. Both receive unwelcome advances, and both are
in two minds about whether to repel or accept them. Both
are imprisoned. In both books there is a disparity in social
class that gives piquancy to the love interest. Both *Pamela*
and *Arcadia* were romances intended chiefly for a female

readership, and both had a healthy dose of the erotic (in both, for example, there is the motif of a disguised or concealed male watching a female undressing). In both books Pamela finally reaps the rewards of her honey-like sweetness and virtue. There is no doubt that the parallel between the two Pamelas was deliberate.

The extent to which mid-eighteenth-century readers would have recognized the coded nature of *Pamela* is uncertain. When the book came out many were in doubt as to how to pronounce the name of the heroine, which seems to argue for a lack of familiarity with *Arcadia*, at least among the mass readership of *Pamela*. In *Pamela* a minor character, Sir Jacob Swynford, says: '"But, *Pamela*? – Did you say? – A *queer* sort of Name! I have heard of it somewhere! – Is it a Christian or a Pagan name?"' Henry Fielding made a joke out of the unfamiliarity of the name in *Joseph Andrews* (1742), when he had one character say: '"They had a Daughter of a very strange Name, Pam□la or Pam□la; some pronounced it one way, and some the other."' Given this, *Pamela* is a bold stroke as a title. It is almost as if Richardson had called his novel *Lapema* or *Malepa*.

Most publishers today would strongly warn an author against publishing a book with an unrecognizable one-word title: there is nothing to draw in book-browsers, and it might be about anything – a foreign destination, a foodstuff, a desert wind. But Richardson was a printer himself, knew his publishers well, and was perhaps willing to be obstinate.

6

Pride and Prejudice (1813)
Persuasion (1817)
Jane Austen

THE titles of Jane Austen's first two published novels have a symmetry it is impossible to ignore. They are *Sense and Sensibility* (1811) and *Pride and Prejudice* (1813). Both feature two opposed abstract nouns, and in doing so they drew on a titling strategy common at the turn of the nineteenth century. Abstract noun titles, either dual or single, were very fashionable, especially as productions of women writers. We have, for example, *Nature and Art* (1796) by Elizabeth Inchbald; *Love and Fashion* (1799) by Fanny Burney; *Self-Control* (1811) and *Discipline* (1814) by Mary Brunton; and *Patronage* (1814) by Maria Edgeworth. We might recall that one of Jane Austen's earliest efforts at prose fiction was called *Love and Freindship* (sic) and that the first draft of *Pride and Prejudice* (completed in 1797) was entitled *First Impressions*. Jane Austen also wrote to her niece Anna in 1814 about her novel, tentatively entitled *Enthusiasm*, saying that such a title was 'something so very superior'.

So in her early career Jane Austen was writing to capture a market, deploying her abstract-noun titles as fashionable bait. But with *Pride and Prejudice* something else was happening under the surface.

Jane Austen was a great admirer of the playwright and novelist Fanny Burney. Burney's first two novels, *Evelina* (1778) and *Cecilia* (1782), were best-sellers, and she went on to have further success with *Camilla* (1796). In *Northanger Abbey* Austen referred to *Cecilia* and *Camilla* as the patterns of achievement in the novel form:

> 'And what are you reading, Miss — ?' 'Oh! It is only a novel!' replies the young lady, while she lays down her book with affected indifference, or momentary shame. 'It is only Cecilia, or Camilla, or Belinda;' or, in short, only some work in which the greatest powers of the mind are displayed, in which the most thorough knowledge of human nature, the happiest delineation of its varieties, the liveliest effusions of wit and humour, are conveyed to the world in the best-chosen language.

In a letter of 1796 Jane talks about an acquaintance, a Miss Fletcher, who admires *Camilla* – this being one of two 'pleasing' aspects of her personality, the other that 'she drinks no cream in her tea' – and in *Persuasion* she has Anne Elliot mention a character from *Cecilia* ('the inimitable Miss Larolles'). And it seems that it was from *Cecilia* that Austen got the title for her best-loved novel. *Cecilia* ends with a paragraph in which the capitalized phrase 'PRIDE and PREJUDICE' recurs three times:

'The whole of this unfortunate business,' said Dr Lyster,
'has been the result of PRIDE and PREJUDICE. Your
uncle, the Dean, began it, by his arbitrary will, as if an
ordinance of his own could arrest the course of nature!
and as if *he* had power to keep alive, by the loan of a
name, a family in the male branch already extinct. Your
father, Mr Mortimer, continued it with the same self-par-
tiality, preferring the wretched gratification of tickling
his ear with a favourite sound, to the solid happiness of
his son with a rich and deserving wife. Yet this, however,
remember; if to PRIDE and PREJUDICE you owe your
miseries, so wonderfully is good and evil balanced,
that to PRIDE and PREJUDICE you will also owe their
termination: for all that I could say to Mr Delvile, either
of reasoning or entreaty, – and I said all I could suggest, and I suggested all a man need wish to hear, – was
totally thrown away, till I pointed out to him his *own*
disgrace, in having a *daughter-in-law* immured in these
mean lodgings!'

Austen, then, was an admirer of Burney, and in many
ways was indebted to her. But as the critic Janet Todd
has pointed out, *Pride and Prejudice* marks an important
departure from the conventions of *Cecilia* – and indeed
from the conventions of the eighteenth-century and early
nineteenth-century 'courtship novel' in general. In *Cecilia*
the 'pride and prejudice' the unhappy lovers encounter are
the pride and prejudice of society against their union. In
Austen's treatment, by contrast, pride and prejudice are
internalized, existing within the breasts of the main characters: Fitzwilliam Darcy is the embodiment of pride, and

Elizabeth Bennet the embodiment of prejudice. This represents a major psychological shift. No longer is the heroine a passive repository of virtue, as in the standard eighteenth-century novel (one might think in this context of Samuel Richardson's *Pamela* and *Clarissa*): Elizabeth Bennet is a heroine of considerable personal charm and wit, but is not without faults. Jane Austen wanted a more rounded heroine. 'Pictures of perfection as you know make me sick and wicked,' she wrote to Fanny Knight in March 1817.

Pride and Prejudice therefore continues the Burney line but introduces new elements. They were new enough to make her more celebrated than any female novelist before George Eliot.

As Austen's career progressed, she discarded the abstract noun title and began to focus on real estate or proper names, as in *Mansfield Park* (1814) and *Emma* (1815).[10] When it came to *Persuasion*, it appears that she decided to return to type, giving us a final abstract noun title.

Except that *Persuasion* was not Jane Austen's choice.

Persuasion was her last complete work (and the only full-length novel for which there exists a written manuscript), and was unpublished and untitled on her death in 1817. Henry and Cassandra Austen brought it out in December of that year, along with another unpublished novel, *Northanger Abbey*. Evidence from Jane's great-niece sug-

---

10 The proper name title was of course rife in the women's literature of the period: we have *Belinda* (1801), *Leonora* (1806) and *Helen* (1834) by Maria Edgeworth; *Emmeline* (1788), *Ethelinde* (1789) and *Celestina* (1791) by Charlotte Smith; and *Henrietta* (1758), *Sophia* (1762) and *Euphemia* (1790) by Charlotte Lennox.

gests that Jane wanted to call the book *The Elliots* but had not made up her mind. Henry and Cassandra were therefore forced to choose something themselves, and went for a nice safe abstract noun title, indicating seriousness of purpose, moral rectitude and philosophical sophistication.

But even though unchosen by the author, *Persuasion*, as a title, was a brilliant stroke. 'Persuasion' is almost a pun, since it contains the meanings of 'influence' and 'opinion', both of which are thematically significant to the novel. (E.g. we can say that Anne Elliot 'succumbed to persuasion' when she refused Captain Wentworth, though secretly, she was 'of another persuasion', i.e. opinion.) The clash between interior worth, interior judgement ('opinion'), on the one hand, and the demands of exterior society on the other ('influence'), is central to the novel. The title *Persuasion* thus functions almost as a double-noun title in itself. It is *Pride and Prejudice* or *Sense and Sensibility* in a smaller package.

7

The Revolt of Islam (1818)
Percy Bysshe Shelley

THE title of Shelley's epic poem – it is 4,800 lines long, the size of a small novel – is quite well known today. As a catchphrase, it has been very popular among op-ed headline-writers, documentary filmmakers, cultural gurus and authors of scholarly papers[11], suggesting, as it does, the clash between Islamic fundamentalism and the crusading West. But these modern echoes have very little to do with Shelley's poem. *The Revolt of Islam* contains barely a mention of Islam (the word occurs once).

The original title of the poem was *Laon and Cythna; or, The Revolution of the Golden City: A Vision of the Nineteenth Century*. It was written while Shelley was living with his young wife Mary at Great Marlow, Buckinghamshire, in 1817. The story is set in Greece, where Laon and Cythna, a young brother and sister, live under the oppressive rule of the Turkish tyrant Othman. Shelley describes their plight in language a little reminiscent of his sonnet 'Ozymandias', written in the same year:

---

11 E.g. *Farewell Israel: Bush, Iran and the Revolt of Islam* by Joel Gilbert; 'The Revolt of Islam' by Bernard Lewis in the *New Yorker*; 'The Revolt of Islam, 1700 to 1993', by Nikki Keddie.

The land in which I lived by a fell bane
Was withered up. Tyrants dwelt side by side,
And stabled in our homes, until the chain
Stifled the captive's cry, and to abide
That blasting curse men had no shame. All vied
In evil, slave and despot; fear with lust
Strange fellowship through mutual hate had tied...

Laon begins to preach sedition, but disaster befalls them both: Cythna is abducted and raped by Othman, and Laon thrown into a foul dungeon where he goes mad. Cythna is also imprisoned, in a cavern by the sea, where she gives birth to Othman's child, but is unexpectedly freed by an earthquake, after which she is rescued by a slave ship. After persuading the slavers to abjure their trade, she journeys to the Golden City (Constantinople) where she restyles herself Laone (in Laon's memory), and begins to preach a gospel of non-violent resistance. Laon, who has also been set free and recovered his wits, joins Laone just as Othman's forces are arriving to crush the fledgling movement. Othman's troops are won over with pacifist rhetoric, but another army arrives, and Laone's supporters are slaughtered. Laone, in the nick of time, rescues Laon on 'a black Tartarian horse of giant frame'. At this point brother and sister surrender themselves to the delights of physical love. They are then captured by Othman and burned alive. In a mystical epilogue they sail to the land of Good, accompanied by Laone's child.

Put like that, the poem seems utterly silly, a Romantic *faux*-oriental romp, with slave-ships, rape, battle, earthquake, incestuous love, gory climax and all. But the exotic events are the cover for something else entirely. The tale of Laon and Cythna is an excuse for the presentation of a remarkable series of ideas that have much in common with earlier libertarian works by Shelley such as *Queen Mab*. Shelley extols notions such as free love, pacifism, vegetarianism and sexual equality (Laone rescues Laon on a black charger, not the other way around); and fundamental to the poem is an attempt to come to terms with the recent failure of the French Revolution. The poem begins:

> When the last hope of trampled France had failed
> Like a brief dream of unremaining glory,
> From visions of despair I rose....

Shelley said in his Preface that its purpose was to try to retrieve from the French experiment whatever was good:

> The panic which, like an epidemic transport, seized
> upon all classes of men during the excesses consequent
> upon the French Revolution, is gradually giving place to
> sanity. It has ceased to be believed that whole genera-
> tions of mankind ought to consign themselves to a
> hopeless inheritance of ignorance and misery, because
> a nation of men who had been dupes and slaves for
> centuries were incapable of conducting themselves with
> the wisdom and tranquillity of freemen so soon as some
> of their fetters were partially loosened.

Shelley was wandering dangerously close to sedition himself, by seeking to account for the excesses of the Revolution. Britain, of course, had been at war with France off and on since 1793, and the Treaty of Paris had only recently been signed. Shelley's attempt to humanize the revolutionaries in 1817 was as if a public figure of our own times had suggested that the Al-Qaeda might have a point.

The poem was published uncensored, but not long afterwards, the publishers, C and J Ollier, began to get cold feet. It was not just the revolutionary sentiments that were worrying. Shelley's poem was very anti-religious. The 1817 version contained several outright polemics against Christianity ('Almighty God his hell on earth has spread!'). There had been a number of recent trials for blasphemous libel – such as those of James Williams and William Hone – which had attracted prison sentences. And the incest-theme was no small matter either. *Laon and Cythna* contained an unambiguous account of brother and sister breathlessly involved in a sexual act:

> What are kisses whose fire clasps
> The failing heart in languishment, or limb
> Twined within limb? or the quick dying gasps
> Of the life meeting, when the faint eyes swim
> Through tears of a wide mist boundless and dim,
> In one caress?

Leigh Hunt's *Story of Rimini* and Byron's *Manfred* had both recently been denounced for their incestuous themes. Leigh Hunt was known to be having an affair with his sister-in-law, and Byron was carrying on with his own half-sister. Shelley too had recently been the object of some scandal, and was reputed to have established a 'seraglio at Marlow'. Ollier decided to suppress the 1817 version, and recalled all the copies he could trace. Shelley was persuaded, very reluctantly, to acquiesce in a new version, which appeared in January 1818. In this expurgated tale, Cythna was now no longer a sister, but an 'orphan' adopted by Laon's family. The anti-Christian rhetoric was also much toned down. A 'Christian priest' in the 1817 version – presented as an Inquisitorial figure, in whose 'breast did hate and guile lie watchful' – was re-styled an 'Iberian' priest; and 'God' throughout was changed to 'Power'. The title too was altered. *Laon and Cythna* drew too much attention to the love-relationship (the incestuous aspect of which had not been entirely extirpated in the new version). *The Revolt of Islam* was a soothing substitute. Strange to modern ears, it was chosen so as *not* to frighten the horses. And it was of very limited relevance to the story. Shelley admitted in a letter of October 13 1817:

> The scene is supposed to be laid in Constantinople and modern Greece, but without much attempt at minute delineation of Mahometan manners. It is, in fact, a tale illustrative of such a revolution as might be supposed to take place in an European nation.

There is no 'revolt of Islam', as such; in fact the true revolt is of free-thought against the forces of institutional religion, whether Islamic or Christian. The Catholic Iberian priest conspires with the Muslim Othman to oppress the unlucky Greeks. As Shelley put it in his preface to the poem, it was intended to achieve

> the awakening of an immense nation from their slavery
> and degradation to a true sense of moral dignity and
> freedom; the bloodless dethronement of their oppres-
> sors, and the unveiling of the religious frauds by which
> they had been deluded into submission.

But this atheistic and libertarian message was seriously weakened in the expurgated version. This has probably contributed to the poem's current obscurity. Few now have heard of the great love of Cythna for Laon. Only the replacement title, an afterthought, lives on.

8

The Mystery of Marie Rogêt (1842)
Edgar Allan Poe

POE has been credited with originating almost every modern literary genre. In the 'Inspector Dupin' tales he pioneered the detective story; in tales such as 'The Masque of the Red Death' and 'The Pit and the Pendulum' he invented what we now call the horror story; and he was certainly an important early practitioner of science fiction in stories such as 'The Unparalleled Adventure of One Hans Pfaal', which describes a journey to the moon. And in 'The Mystery of Marie Rogêt' he wrote the first real-life murder mystery – that is, the first detective story ever to be based on a real homicide.

In 1841 Poe had caused quite a stir with 'The Murders in the Rue Morgue' – a story in which (spoiler here) 'the orangutan did it' – and needed a follow-up. He decided to feature, once again, the ingenious C. Auguste Dupin, freelance criminal consultant and precursor, of course, of Sherlock Holmes. The trouble was that he had no plot. Then New York supplied one.

In the summer of 1841 the city was agog at the murder of Mary Cecilia Rogers, a sales-girl in a tobacco-shop. Mary was a minor celebrity, noted for her beauty and charm. She had been specifically engaged as a fascinating butterfly for gentlemen customers to flirt with; her shop was frequented by journalists and writers such as Washington Irving and James Fenimore Cooper. On the morning of Sunday, July 25, 1841, she left home and did not return. Three days later her body was found floating in the Hudson, off Hoboken. She appeared to have been beaten, and a cord was wrapped around her neck. The murder was attributed to gang violence (there were reports that Mary had been gang-raped), but there were no compelling leads, and after several weeks of feverish speculation the case was dropped. Then Poe came forward. On June 4, 1842 he wrote to the Boston publisher George Roberts saying that he was going to 'enter into a very long and rigorous analysis' of the case in an attempt to solve it. His method would be 'altogether novel in literature,' since he was going to cast light on the murder through a fictional treatment of its details. But he failed to convince Roberts that the result would be either literature or investigative journalism, and eventually he sold the story to another journal, *Snowden's Ladies' Companion*, which ran it in three instalments from November 1842.

This tale was 'The Mystery of Marie Rogêt', and it was billed as 'the sequel to 'The Murders in the Rue Morgue'. It transposed the crime-scene from New York to Paris, and featured C. Auguste Dupin as the investigator. Mary Rogers became 'Marie Rogêt', and instead of a cigar sales-girl she became a perfume sales-girl. Her death by water took place in the Seine, not the Hudson. Otherwise the facts were the same. Poe introduced the tale with an almost audible licking of the lips:

> The atrocity of this murder, (for it was at once evident that murder had been committed,) the youth and beauty of the victim, and, above all, her previous notoriety, conspired to produce intense excitement in the minds of the sensitive Parisians. I can call to mind no similar occurrence producing so general and so intense an effect.

He presented the case as one of true crime, and tried to account for the strange similarity between Marie's case and that of Mary Rogers:

> [I]n what I relate it will be seen that between the fate of the unhappy Mary Cecilia Rogers, so far as that fate is known, and the fate of one Marie Rogêt up to a certain epoch in her history, there has existed a parallel in the contemplation of whose wonderful exactitude the reason becomes embarrassed.

What came next was an examination of the facts of the murder, all gleaned from the yellow journalism of the previous year. Poe dwelt at length on matters such as the buoyancy of corpses in water, whether 'Marie' had drowned or been strangled, whether 'Marie' had had any secret sexual life, whether the clothes that had been found in a thicket had been planted by the murderers, whether they had been deliberately torn to make it seem as if there had been a struggle, whether the motive was rape, whether it was by a gang (the popular view), and so on. All of these details derived from the Mary Rogers case, and Poe had to invent very little. But then there was a development. Before the last instalment of the story could be published, an inn-keeper, one Mrs Loss, confessed on her deathbed that Mary's death was the result of a botched abortion. The *New York Tribune* of 18 November 1842 carried the story:

> On the Sunday of Miss Rogers' disappearance she came
> to her [Mrs. Loss's] house from this city in company
> with a young physician, who undertook to procure
> for her a premature delivery. While in the hands of the
> physician she died, and a consultation was then held as
> to the disposal of her body. It was finally taken at night
> by the son of Mrs. Loss and sunk in the river where it
> was found. Her clothes were first tied up in a bundle
> and sunk in a pool [...] but it was afterward thought they
> were not safe there, and they were accordingly taken
> and scattered through the woods as they were found.

Mrs Loss's deputation was not widely believed, and New York public opinion continued to suspect a cover-up. Two other women, Mrs Restell and Mrs Costello, were known to be involved in the procurement of abortions, and in February 1846 there was a fracas outside the house of Mrs Costello, the mob crying: 'Haul her out!', 'Where's the thousand children murdered in this house?' and 'Who murdered Mary Rogers?' But Poe was forced to incorporate some of the new details in the third and final instalment of the tale, published in February 1843. He left his conclusion extremely vague, however, and there was no 'solution' as such. A 'man of dark complexion,' a naval officer, was implicated, but it was not much of a lead.

No convictions were ever brought, and the case remains unsolved.

'The Mystery of Marie Rogêt' sits uneasily with the two other Dupin tales, that is, 'The Murders in the Rue Morgue' (notable for its astonishing climax) and 'The Purloined Letter' (which gains its effect through a singular piece of psychology). In comparison, 'The Mystery of Marie Rogêt' meanders tediously and is fatally fudged. There is no thrilling climax and the crime is never solved. In one way, though, it had a shaping influence over the development of the detective genre. The particular variety of detective fiction that tends to dominate today is so-called 'crime fiction'. In the crime fiction of James Patterson, Val McDermid or Karin Slaughter, there is the same preoccupation with sexual violence and the brutal deaths of women. The battered and abused corpses of once-beautiful females, in a lineal descent from Poe's Marie Rogêt – shading, in modern times, into a preoccupation with paedophilia, torture and mutilation – are firmly settled in the mainstream. Poe said in his essay 'The Philosophy of Composition' (1846) that 'the death [...] of a beautiful woman is unquestionably the most poetical topic in the world.' And with Poe as the true progenitor of the detective story, we can see Sherlock Holmes, with his gentlemanly conundra about missing jewels or the best way out of a locked room, as a sort of quaint diversion from the main current. The morbolatrous, woman-haunted Poe reaches out to us from beyond the grave and continues to fashion our most delicious nightmares.

9

The House of the Seven Gables (1851)
Nathaniel Hawthorne

ON the waterfront at Salem, Massachusetts, is an ancient
wooden house that would not look out of place in a horror
film. Tall, weathered, clapboarded, it has seven gables (tri-
angular roof-ends) pointing spikily into the air. It would
be a remarkable house even if it were not for the fact that
it boasts two superlatives: it is America's oldest surviv-
ing mansion house, dating to 1668, and is the country's
most famous literary house, the inspiration for Nathaniel Hawthorne's novel *The House of the Seven Gables*. It is
part of a complex of seventeenth and eighteenth-century
buildings in Salem which, as a whole, is redolent of – and
indeed actively associated by its curators with – such
things as the Salem witchcraft trials, the American Revolution, the 'Underground Railway' of escaping slaves,
and the maritime trade with the West Indies. It is a nexus
of everything American, colonial and historical. Yet the
house itself is a fake.

It's not really surprising that people allow themselves
to be fooled. Hawthorne himself took the lead, identifying

the house as the original of the book in a letter to a friend, Horace Conolly, of May 1840. Hawthorne often visited the house, which was owned by his cousin Susannah Ingersoll (who he nicknamed 'the Duchess'). He wrote:

> The day after the great storm in March, I went with David Roberts to make a call on the Duchess at the old house in Turner Street, to learn how she weathered the gale. I had a more than ordinary pleasant visit, and among other things, in speaking of the old house, she said it has had in the history of its changes and altera-tions Seven Gables. The expression was new and struck me very forcibly; I think I shall make something of it. I expressed a wish to go all over the house; she assented and I repaired to the Attic, and there was no corner or dark hole did not peep into. I could readily make out five gables, and on returning to the parlour l inquired where the two remaining gables were placed. The infor-mation I received was that the remaining gables were on the north side, and that when Col. Turner became the owner of the house, he removed the 'lean to' on which were the missing gables, and made amends by placing three gables on the L or addition which he made on the south side of the house; the mark of beams still remains in the studding to show precisely where they were.

After Susannah Ingersoll's death in 1858 the house changed hands several times. In 1908 it was acquired by Caroline Emmerton. By this time the house had only three gables, and Emmerton, partly because of the number of literary pilgrims now washing up against its doors, decided to add four more to restore it to its true seven-gabled state. Under

her direction the house was transformed from a rather unremarkable, if large and old, dwelling, to something more
akin to the colonial Gothic monstrosity of Hawthorne's
novel. She added, at street level, a penny shop (like the
one in the novel), a magnificent new central chimney, and
a secret staircase. The result, when opened to the public,
proved an enormous tourist draw. In the first year, admis-
sion fees amounted to $2,000, and by 1924 around 30,000
tourists were visiting annually.

The house was marketed very much as the original
house of the novel. The characters of the novel – Hepzibah
Pyncheon, her brother Clifford, and cousin Phoebe – were
each allotted separate rooms in the house, and guides
were taught to tell visitors: 'This was Miss Hepzibah's
bedroom... everything here is just as Hawthorne saw it
last. All that we do is to keep it well dusted. We never
move or disturb anything.' The success of the venture
was so great – the profits being funnelled into a charity
that Emmerton had set up for newly-arrived immigrants
– that several nearby houses were bought up and became
part of a new organization, the House of the Seven Gables
Settlement Association. It was now a fully-modern tourist
trap, supplying food, lodging, antiques, gifts, and tea in
the newly-landscaped garden. A special copy of the novel
was printed for visitors to buy as a souvenir. The final
touch came when Hawthorne's birthplace was added to
the complex in 1958. He had actually been born in nearby
Union St, but the house was purchased by the Association, taken apart and re-built brick by brick on site so as

to be within the grounds of the House of the Seven Gables Settlement (and near the gift shop).

Disneyfication, yes: but why not? The link in the letter was solid enough, and all Emmerton had done was to 'restore' the gables. Unfortunately Hawthorne, despite what he had said in his letter, rather muddied the waters in other writings. In his Preface to the novel he was keen to distance the text from any actual physical location:

> The reader may perhaps choose to assign an actual locality to the imaginary events of this narrative. If permitted by the historical connection, – which, though slight, was essential to his plan, – the author would very willingly have avoided anything of this nature. Not to speak of other objections, it exposes the romance to an inflexible and exceedingly dangerous species of criticism, by bringing his fancy-pictures almost into positive contact with the realities of the moment. [...] He trusts not to be considered as unpardonably offending by laying out a street that infringes upon nobody's private rights, and appropriating a lot of land which had no visible owner, and building a house of materials long in use for constructing castles in the air. [...] He would be glad, therefore, if – especially in the quarter to which he alludes – the book may be read strictly as a Romance, having a great deal more to do with the clouds overhead than with any portion of the actual soil of the County of Essex.[12]

And the general climate of critical opinion before Emmerton's restoration was with Hawthorne. In the late nineteenth

---

12 Essex being a county of Massachusetts.

century there were several rivals for the 'original' house of the book. The author of the foreword to an 1879 edition of the *House of the Seven Gables* wrote:

> Hundreds of pilgrims annually visit a house in Salem, belonging to one branch of the Ingersoll family of that place, which is stoutly maintained to have been the model for Hawthorne's visionary dwelling. Others have supposed that the now vanished house of the identical Philip English, whose blood, as we have already noticed, became mingled with that of the Hawthornes, supplied the pattern; and still a third building, known as the Curwen mansion, has been declared the only genuine establishment. Notwithstanding persistent popular belief, the authenticity of all these must positively be denied; although it is possible that isolated reminiscences of all three may have blended with the ideal image in the mind of Hawthorne.

The House of the Seven Gables by these readings is a creation of the mind, not a place. There is no 'real' House of the Seven Gables. Hawthorne sat down to write the book a good eleven years after he had made that visit in May 1840, after all. Soaked as he was in the history of Salem, he was able to pour into the book much else of the architecture, customs and manners of bygone times; he was not restricted to the appearance and contents of a single house. In any case, looking at the original letter, Hawthorne does not say that the *house* was the inspiration for the novel – he says that the *expression* was the inspiration for the novel: 'The expression was new and struck me very forcibly; I think

I shall make something of it.' Novels are made of words, and the novel *The House of the Seven Gables* has rather different purposes to the physical House of the Seven Gables. Each tells a story, and each is in its way a confection: the novel is a family drama revolving around an ancient family curse, and the physical House of the Seven Gables recounts a national drama of settlement, origins and heritage.

10

Aunt Phillis's Cabin (1852)
Mary Henderson Eastman

IT'S perhaps not too difficult to guess how *Aunt Phillis's Cabin* got its title. Published in 1852, it was a response to one of the best-selling novels of the nineteenth century: *Uncle Tom's Cabin* by Harriet Beecher Stowe.

One can hardly overestimate the impact of *Uncle Tom's Cabin*. Stowe's book, telling the story of the saintly slave Tom, 'sold down the river' to a new master, who abuses him and finally beats him to death, sold hundreds of thousands of copies within the first year of publication, becoming less a literary than a social and political phenomenon.[13] It crystallized Northern opinion against slavery and was an important step in the path that led America into Civil War. A 1911 biography of Stowe described a meeting between Stowe and Abraham Lincoln, in which Lincoln remarked: 'So you're the little woman who wrote the book that made

---

13 Many had a low opinion of Stowe's literary skills. William Dean Howells said cattily in his *Literary Friends and Acquaintances*: 'As for the author of "Uncle Tom's Cabin" her syntax was such a snare to her that it sometimes needed the combined skill of all the proof-readers and the assistant editor to extricate her. Of course, nothing was ever written into her work, but in changes of diction, in correction of solecisms, in transposition of phrases, the text was largely rewritten on the margin of her proofs.'

this great war!' And as well as inflaming America, *Uncle Tom's Cabin* was a best-seller in Britain, and was translated into a myriad of languages worldwide. Such was its global penetration that the psychiatrist Richard von Krafft-Ebing mentioned it in his *Psychopathia Sexualis* (1886), quoting a patient who derived gratification from the thought of being physically chastised:

> The thought of slavery had something exciting in it for me, alike whether from the standpoint of master or servant. That one man could possess, sell or whip another, caused me intense excitement; and in reading 'Uncle Tom's Cabin' (which I read at about the beginning of puberty) I had erections.

But reactions were not so universally positive. In the Southern States, as might be expected, there was outrage. Stowe was denounced as a sentimentalizing propagandist who knew nothing of real conditions in the South and had never bothered to visit a plantation. Others derided her as a woman writer meddling in male politics: John R Thompson of the *Southern Literary Messenger*, the most influential Southern editor of his day, snorted that Stowe 'would place woman on a footing of political equality with man, and causing her to look beyond the office for which she was created – the high and holy office of maternity – would engage her in the administration of public affairs; thus handing over the State to the perilous protection of diaper diplomatists and wet-nurse politicians.'

In the wake of *Uncle Tom's Cabin* there were dozens of novels published to present the pro-slavery side of the case. This body of work is now known as 'Anti-Tom literature' or 'Plantation literature'. In a typical offering, *The Planter's Northern Bride* (1854) by Caroline Hentz, it is the Abolitionists who are pompous, arrogant and hard-hearted, so much so that one slave flees from the North across the Ohio River back into a benign servitude. Other titles of the 'Anti-Tom' boom (a very large proportion by women) included *Ellen, or, The Fanatic's Daughter* by Mrs. V.G. Cowdin; *Antifanaticism, A Tale of the South* by Martha Haines Butt; *The Lofty and the Lowly, or, Good in All and None All-Good* by Maria McIntosh; *The Sword and the Distaff* by William Gilmore Simms; *Liberia, or, Mr Peyton's Experiments* by Sarah Hale; *The Ebony Idol* by Mrs. G.M. Flanders; *The Black Gauntlet, A Tale of Plantation Life in South Carolina* by Mary Schoolcraft; *Frank Freeman's Barber Shop* by the Rev. Baynard R. Hall; and *The North and the South, or, Slavery and Its Contrasts* by Caroline Rush. Some echoed in their titles the title of the book that had incensed them. Among these were *Uncle Robin, in His Cabin in Virginia, and Tom Without One in Boston* by JW Page; *The Cabin and Parlor, or, Slaves and Masters* by J Thornton Randolph; and *Aunt Phillis's Cabin, or, Southern Life As It Is* by Mary Henderson Eastman.

Aunt Phillis's Cabin was one of the earliest and most successful 'Anti-Tom' novels, selling a reported 18,000 copies in the first few weeks of publication. Its author, Mary Henderson Eastman, was famous for her travels in the frontier lands of the West, and had already published one successful book, *Dahcotah: Or, Life and Legends of the Sioux around Fort Snelling* (1849). Some measure of her energy can be seen in the fact that her riposte to *Uncle Tom's Cabin* was published in the same year as Stowe's novel – 1852.[14] *Aunt Phillis's Cabin* is set in Virginia, and features a compassionate plantation-owner, Mr Weston, his daughter Anna, and a cast of Black characters rejoicing in their slavery, among them Aunt Phillis, a pious middle-aged slave, and Uncle Bacchus, her tippling husband. Aunt Phillis is presented as a model of dignified Negro womanhood, sober, industrious and wise:

> Her neatly white-washed cottage was enclosed by a wooden fence in good condition – her little garden laid out with great taste [...] The room in which Phillis ironed, was not encumbered with much furniture. Her ironing-table occupied a large part of its centre, and in the ample fireplace was blazing a fire great enough to cook a repast for a moderate number of giants. Behind the back door stood a common pine bedstead, with an enormous bed upon it. [...] There was no cooking done in this room, there being a small shed for that purpose, back of the house; not a spot of grease dimmed the whiteness of the floors, and order reigned supreme, marvellous to relate! where a descendant of Afric's daughters presided.

Phillis is so happy with her cabin that she refuses freedom even when it is offered her. She dies at the book's end, in a

---

14 *Uncle Tom's Cabin* was originally published as a magazine serial in 1851 before appearing as a book in 1852, but Eastman's rapid response is still impressive.

deliberate parallel to Tom's death in *Uncle Tom's Cabin*. At the moment of her death Phillis uses her presence centre-stage to say she has no regrets about how she has spent her life, i.e. enslaved.

Aunt Phillis's Cabin was thus intended as a mirror to *Uncle Tom's Cabin*, providing, as mirrors do, a reversed image of the subject. As in *Uncle Tom's Cabin*, *Aunt Phillis's Cabin* set up characters representative of different sides of the North-South argument, and conducted lengthy dialogues between them in an attempt to establish that slavery is the natural condition of the Black races. Where Stowe had said that the cruellest aspect of slavery was the splitting up of families when slaves were sold, Eastman countered that this was 'very uncommon' and that masters who practised it were held in 'utter abhorrence' by their white neighbours. Where Stowe had told lurid stories of burnings and whippings, Eastman said that such things were unknown, and perhaps originated in sly jokes told by Southerners to shock credulous Northerners. Perhaps the most striking reversal in the two books was the differing use of Biblical authority. Harriet Beecher Stowe had used Christian teachings to argue against the institution of slavery; Mary Henderson Eastman used them to argue for it:

> A writer on Slavery has no difficulty in tracing back its
> origin. There is also the advantage of finding it, with
> its continued history, and the laws given by God to
> govern his own institution, in the Holy Bible. Neither
> profane history, tradition, nor philosophical research are
> required to prove its origin or existence; though they, as

all things must, come forward to substantiate the truth
of the Scriptures. God, who created the human race,
willed they should be holy like himself. Sin was committed, and the curse of sin, death, was induced: other
punishments were denounced [sic] for the perpetration
of particular crimes – the shedding of man's blood for
murder, and the curse of slavery. The mysterious reasons
that here influenced the mind of the Creator it is not ours
to declare.

The passage Eastman leans on the heaviest is that in Genesis, in which Ham, Noah's son, sees his father's nakedness;
as a punishment for this, Ham's son Canaan is given as a
servant to the other sons of Noah. The African continent,
being peopled by the descendants of Ham, is thus fair
game:

However inexplicable may be the fact that God would
appoint the curse of continual servitude on a portion of
his creatures, will any one *dare*, with the Bible open in
his hands, to say the fact does not exist? It is not ours to
decide *why* the Supreme Being acts! We may observe his
dealings with man, but we may not ask, until he reveals
it, Why hast thou thus done?

Nor were Christ or Paul Abolitionists. Christ alluded to slavery but did not denounce it. Paul took active steps to restore
a slave, Onesimus, to his master. Eastman concluded:

Turning aside the institutions and commands of God,
treading under foot the love of country, despising the
laws of nature and the nation, [Abolitionism] is dead to

every feeling of patriotism and brotherly kindness; full
of strife and pride, strewing the path of the slave with
thorns and of the master with difficulties, accomplishing
nothing good, forever creating disturbance.

In the contest between *Uncle Tom's Cabin* and *Aunt Phillis's Cabin* we know who the victor was. *Uncle Tom's Cabin* outsold *Aunt Phillis's Cabin*; it backed the winner in the Civil War; anything opposed to its anti-slavery message is anathema to the modern mind. But the two novels now seem like a pair of grappling dinosaurs that have disappeared together into a tar pit. The protests they existed to embody have died away, to be replaced by new concerns about race and politics. Stowe and Eastman's contemporaries, writers such as Nathaniel Hawthorne, Herman Melville or Louisa May Alcott, are still read today for pleasure. But nowhere, outside university departments, does anyone read for pleasure *Uncle Tom's Cabin* or its imitator, *Aunt Phillis's Cabin*.

11

The Confidence-Man (1857)
Herman Melville

THE Confidence-Man has been hailed as Melville's second-greatest book after *Moby-Dick*.[15] Literary theorists have
pounced on it with delight, investigating it as an exercise in
textual subversion or an inquiry into the art of fiction itself.
It certainly exhibits a precociously modern sensibility, featuring a plot of multiple ambiguities, as well as characters
who seem to merge into one another. Jack Kerouac said:
'Melville in *The Confidence-Man* is the strangest voice ever
heard in America', and added that it was great book to
read while stoned. It was also Melville's swan-song, since
he published no other fiction after it, even though he lived
on for another thirty-four years.

The Confidence-Man is set on a single day, April 1 (April
Fool's Day), 1857. It takes place on a Mississippi steamer, the
Fidèle, as she journeys from St Louis to New Orleans, and its
central character is a trickster who, in various guises, fleeces
his fellow passengers, generally of small amounts of money. A

---

15 To be fair, several of Melville's books have been hailed as his second-greatest after *Moby-Dick*.

major problem for the reader is how many 'confidence-men' there actually are in the book. Some readers have counted seven, some eight; some include the narrator himself, making nine. Neither is it clear whether all these confidence-men are really the same person, or are somehow avatars of one another. The first 'confidence-man' to appear is a deaf-mute who carries a slate on which verses from St Paul are written. Then, after a quick costume-change, he is a crippled beggar, 'Black Guinea'. Then he is John Ringman, 'the man with the weed,' in mourning for his dead wife. Then he is a 'man in gray' who solicits contributions to the Seminole Widow and Orphan Asylum. Then he is 'the president and transfer-agent of the Black Rapids Coal Company,' then a herb-doctor, and afterwards 'a Philosophical Intelligence Officer'. Finally, in the most sustained performance, he is a 'cosmopolitan', who manages, after a session of logico-philosophical jousting, to bilk the ship's barber out of the price of a haircut. His patter usually hangs on the nature of 'confidence':

> 'For, comparatively inexperienced as you are, my dear young friend, did you never observe how little, very little, confidence, there is? I mean between man and man – more particularly between stranger and stranger. In a sad world it is the saddest fact. Confidence! I have sometimes almost thought that confidence is fled; that confidence is the New Astrea – emigrated – vanished – gone.' Then softly sliding nearer, with the softest air, quivering down and looking up, 'Could you now, my dear young sir, under such circumstances, by way of experiment, simply have confidence in *me*?'

In other places his hucksterism is closer to that of the classic real-estate bunko artist:

> You wouldn't like to be concerned in the New Jerusalem, would you?'
>
>   'New Jerusalem?'
>
>   'Yes, the new and thriving city, so called, in northern Minnesota. It was originally founded by certain fugitive Mormons. Hence the name. It stands on the Mississippi. Here, here is the map,' producing a roll. 'There – there, you see are the public buildings – here the landing – there the park – yonder the botanic gardens – and this, this little dot here, is a perpetual fountain, you understand. You observe there are twenty asterisks. Those are for the lyceums. They have lignum-vitae rostrums.'
>
>   'And are all these buildings now standing?'
>
>   'All standing – bona fide.'

The confidence-man is a fellow of lively fantasy, ready to talk on any subject, however abstruse. He is a master of disorientation, or misdirection, veering from emollient appeal to unsettling attack. He always brings the talk finally to questions of confidence, its meaning, importance and definition – before asking for money.

The book's ending is as baffling as anything in it. The confidence-man blows out a lamp and escorts an old man to his stateroom: 'Something further may follow of this Masquerade,' the narrator says. But the sequel, if any was intended, never materialized. Melville's career had long since fallen into a terminal slump. The author was only ever admired for his tales of South Seas adventure, such as *Typee* or *Omoo*; his later, more complex works, such as *Moby-Dick* or *Pierre*, were greeted with indifference or hostility. He told Nathaniel Hawthorne in 1856 that he had 'made up his mind to be annihilated,' and when *The Confidence-Man* appeared in 1857 – on April 1, 1857, the very day on which the book itself was set – it was mauled by reviewers, some of whom doubted whether it was even a novel. It sold pitifully, and its US publishers chose the moment to go into liquidation. Melville then gave up writing fiction. He earned a living lecturing for a while, and in 1866 took a job at the New York Custom House. He retired in 1885 and died in 1891, almost completely forgotten as a writer. Critical acclaim would only come many years after his death.

The title *The Confidence-Man* does not seem at all unusual to us – we are used to the term 'confidence' in phrases such as 'confidence-man', 'confidence-trick', 'confidence-game', and in its short form as 'con-man', 'con-trick', 'con-game', 'con-artist', or simply 'con' – but in the 1850s the very idea of a 'confidence-man' was very new. The first appearance in print of the phrase was only eight years earlier, in 1849, to describe the activities of a swindler, William Thompson. The *New York Herald* of July 11,1849 described his method as follows:

> Accosting a well-dressed gentleman in the street, the 'Confidence Man', in a familiar manner, and with an easy nonchalance, worthy of Chesterfield, would playfully put the inquiry – 'Are you really disposed to put any confidence in me?' This interrogatory, thus put, generally met an affirmative answer... 'Well, then,' continues the 'Confidence Man', 'just lend me your watch

till to-morrow!' The victim, already in the snare of the
fowler, complies, with a grin; and, jokingly receiving one
of Tobias' best, the 'Confidence Man' disappears around
the corner.

In the novel the formula 'Are you really disposed to put
any confidence in me?' becomes 'Could you now, my dear,
under such circumstances, by way of experiment, simply
have confidence in *me*?' If the answer was yes, the inevitable response was: 'Prove it. Let me have twenty dollars.'
William Thompson, like the confidence-man of the novel,
was a chimera, representing himself as 'Samuel Williams',
'Samuel Willis', 'Samuel Thompson' or 'Samuel Thomas'.
His main concern, as in the novel, was whether his victims felt confident in him; the matter of money or a watch
was seemingly secondary. In both cases the 'mark' was
overwhelmed by argument – the *Herald* report said that
the 'Confidence Man' possessed 'the gift of speech to
such a degree that sensible men – yes, men of business
– have parted with watch and money'. Both the original
confidence-man and his fictional echo used the device of
pretending acquaintance with their victims in order to
establish 'confidence'.

Melville would almost certainly have heard of the real
confidence-man. He was in New York that month, July
1849, working on his novel *White Jacket*. The confidence-
man affair was in several of the papers – the *Tribune*, the
Knickerbocker, *The Merchant's Ledger* – and in at least one
journal to which Melville subscribed, *Literary World*. The
correspondences in theme and phraseology make William

Thompson, the first ever confidence-man, the undoubted prototype, and the source of Melville's title.

There is a further odd circumstance. In the following summer, of 1850, a man was unmasked as a Herman Melville impersonator. The *New York Journal* of July reported:

> It appears that some individual ambitious of notoriety has become enamoured of the good name and reputation of [...] Herman Melville [...] and has been so far successful in his attempts to pass himself off for that gentleman, in remote parts of Georgia and North Carolina, that persons near the scene of his exploits have been induced to correspond with [...] Mr Melville's publishers for the purpose of getting reliable information on the subject of this stranger's claims to be the author of Mr Melville's books. It is believed by many that Herman Melville is the assumed name of the author of *Typee*, &c. This is not the fact. Herman Melville is the real name of the writer of those works.

Confusion tended to swirl around Melville. As noted above, many people apparently believed that 'Herman Melville' was a nom-de-plume. The *Dublin University Magazine* in 1856 stated it as a fact, adding that it probably flowed from 'the mystification which this remarkable author dearly loves to indulge in from the first page to the last of his works'.

These speculations were current just as Melville was writing *The Confidence-Man*. Perhaps the book can be considered not only as a meditation on identity but a meditation on the author's own identity. Was Melville, in his own self-estimation, in 1855-57 still the popular writer of tales of the South Seas – or was that Melville dead and buried, having been replaced by an impersonating Melville, the ignored and unsuccessful author of changelings such as *Moby-Dick* or *Pierre*? Or was Melville no author at all? After 1857 Melville seems to have answered that question. The real Melville, for the last third of his life, was a customs house official. The publication of *The Confidence-Man* was the occasion of Melville's own terminal crisis of confidence.

12

The Woman in White (1860)
Wilkie Collins

THE Woman in White was Wilkie Collins's first unques-
tionable smash hit, rocketing him into the authorial
firmament alongside Dickens and Thackeray. Published in
serial form in the twopenny newspaper *All the Year Round*,
it caused the sort of cross-media sensation that *Pamela* had
in the previous century (see chapter 5). It spawned stage-
plays, dances (the *Woman in White* waltz), *Woman in White*
perfumes, *Woman in White* hats and *Woman in White* cloaks;
Prince Albert was a *Woman in White* addict, and Gladstone
missed a night at the theatre reading it. It was even credited
with inaugurating a new fictional genre, the so-called 'sensation' novel, which dealt with shocking themes such as
adultery, bigamy, kidnapping, false imprisonment, seduc-
tion, madness and death, all taking place in the bosom of
the family. In the sensation novel, as in the films of Alfred
Hitchcock, murder began at home.

The plot of *The Woman in White* is highly convoluted, but
may be simplified as follows. Walter Hartright is a London drawing teacher who lands a job teaching at a country

house in Cumberland. The night before he is due to take up his post, he encounters a mysterious woman in the middle of a deserted street:

> There, in the middle of the broad bright high-road –
> there, as if it had that moment sprung out of the earth or
> dropped from the heaven – stood the figure of a solitary
> Woman, dressed from head to foot in white garments,
> her face bent in grave inquiry on mine, her hand point-
> ing to the dark cloud over London, as I faced her.

She begs Walter for help – she has met with an unspeci-fied 'accident' – and he esquires her to a cab. She departs, kissing his hand. Still vibrating from this adventure, Wal-ter goes to Cumberland to take up his post, and meets his new employers: the eccentric invalid Frederick Fairlie, Fairlie's beautiful niece Laura and her ugly (but virtuous and intelligent) half-sister Marian. Being a superficial fel-low, Hartright falls in love with Laura rather than Marian, but Laura is engaged to the wicked Sir Percival Glyde, and soon marries him. Sir Percival, by an extraordinary coin-cidence, has been involved in the imprisonment of the Woman in White in an asylum; her real name is Anne Cath-erick and she is yet another half-sister of Laura. Anne dies, and with the aid of the diabolical Count Fosco, Sir Percival switches the identities of the two half-sisters, imprisoning Laura in the asylum under the name of Anne Catherick. Walter finally rescues her and all ends happily.

The eerie encounter with Anne, enshrouded in white and pleading for help, is the book's dramatic core, the event from which all else flows. Dickens said that it was one of the two greatest dramatic scenes ever written (the other was in Carlyle's *French Revolution*). It seems to have been drawn from real life.

The story of the 'real' Woman in White first pops up in a book called *The Life and Letters of John Everett Millais*, published in 1899 by John Guille Millais, the son of the painter. The relevant passage is as follows:

> One night in the fifties Millais was returning home to Gower Street from one of the many parties held under Mrs Collins's hospitable roof in Hanover Terrace, and, in accordance with the usual practice of the two brothers, Wilkie and Charles, they accompanied him on his homeward walk through the dimly-lit, and in those days semi-rural, roads and lanes of North London... It was a beautiful moonlight night in the summer time, and as the three friends walked along chatting gaily together, they were suddenly arrested by a piercing scream coming from the garden of a villa close at hand. It was evidently the cry of a woman in distress; and while pausing to consider what they should do, the iron gate leading to the garden was dashed open, and from it came the figure of a young and very beautiful woman dressed in flowing white robes that shone in the moonlight. She seemed to float rather than to run in their direction, and, on coming up to the three young men, she paused for a moment in an attitude of supplication and terror. Then, seeming to recollect herself, she suddenly moved on and vanished in the shadows cast upon the road.
>
> 'What a lovely woman!' was all Millais could say. 'I must see who she is and what's the matter,' said Wilkie

Collins, as, without another word, he dashed off after her. His two companions waited in vain for his return, and next day, when they met again, he seemed indisposed to talk of his adventure. They gathered from him, however, that he had come up with the lovely fugitive and heard from her own lips the history of her life and the cause of her sudden flight. She was a young lady of good birth and position, who had accidentally fallen into the hands of a man living in a villa in Regent's Park. There for many months he kept her prisoner under threats of violence and mesmeric influence of so alarming a character that she dared not attempt to escape, until, in sheer desperation, she fled from the brute, who, with a poker in his hand, threatened to dash her brains out. Her subsequent history, interesting as it is, is not for these pages.

Not for these pages? Why not? The answer can only be that the truth was too scandalous. Wilkie, after collaring his Woman in White, lived with her for the rest of his life. She was Caroline Graves, and she became his mistress.

Caroline Graves was a carpenter's daughter, and she and Wilkie lived together from 1858. Marriage was never a possibility, due partly to the difficulty Wilkie had in reconciling his family to the liaison, but chiefly to his aversion to matrimony under any circumstances. Dickens knew all about the pair (Dickens was himself at the time involved in an illicit affair with the actress Ellen Ternan), as did most of Wilkie's friends, but Caroline's existence was concealed from the rest of the outside world. And it is this aura of mystery and obfuscation that seems to have influenced the passage above. Because it is quite possibly a fabrication.

The chief problem with the account is that it was composed in the 1890s, four decades after the events it was supposed to describe. By then all the participants – Wilkie, Charles, Caroline and Millais – were dead. Catherine Peters, Wilkie's biographer, calls it a 'sensational farrago' and says it likely originated as 'a piece of foolery designed to cover the less exciting and certainly less acceptable reality'. Wilkie *may* have released Caroline from some sort of onerous existence, but probably not in the manner described. For one thing, there is good evidence to show that when they first met she was running a marine store, a sort of Victorian second-hand shop. And there is no independent evidence of any unnamed mesmerist.

And to further confuse things, there is one other famous account of the genesis of the title. This time it is from an interview with Wilkie conducted in 1877 in *The World* newspaper. In this account Wilkie, fully a third of the way through the novel, had not yet decided on a title. Seeking inspiration he went for a walk:

> He walked for several hours on the cliffs between Kingsgate and Bleak House, and smoked an entire case of cigars, striving for a title, but with a barren result. As the sun went down the novelist threw himself on the grass, contemplating the North Foreland lighthouse, and, being hipped and weary, looked by no means lovingly on that hideous edifice. Savagely biting the end of his last cigar he apostrophised the building, standing coldly

and stiffly in the evening light, 'You are ugly and stiff
and awkward; you know you are: as stiff and as weird
as my white woman. White woman! – woman in white!
The title, by Jove!'

But this account also seems to have more than a tinge of
romance. The earliest manuscripts show that he had the
title from the beginning, and the phrase 'the woman in
white' actually appears several times in the first few pages
of the book, when Walter encounters Anne Catherick. It
seems impossible that he could only have stumbled on the
title after writing a third of the book; it seems to have been
in his mind from the first. And so, titularly speaking, we
are thrown back into limbo. Except...

As was pointed out by Clyde K Hyder in 1939, the
theme, plot and title of *The Woman in White* may all derive
from a book published in French in 1808, *Recueil des causes
célèbres*, by Maurice-Méjan, which Wilkie is known to have
read in 1856. Among the various *causes* of the book is the
story of one Madame de Douhault, who was imprisoned
by her brother under the name of 'Blainville' in the Salt-
pêtrière infirmary so that he could seize her estates. She
was finally released by friends, but was unable to prove
her true identity, and died in poverty. At one point in the
narrative it is mentioned that a white dress she was wearing when she was incarcerated was restored to her on her
release.

So this, rather than any of the mythmaking that Wilkie
loved to indulge in, seems to have been the actual origin of
The Woman in White.

Considered purely as a title, *The Woman in White* is one with the stamp of perfection. Dickens wrote in 1859: 'I have not the slightest doubt that The Woman in White is the name of names, and the title of titles.' It is partly the alliteration, of course, but also the invocation of white and its connotations of the spectral, the virginal, the deathly, the tubercular, the terrifying, that clinched its appeal. Subsequent imitators who wrote novels featuring women in red, women in black or women in grey – and there were many – could never really compete. White was the colour of sensation.

13

Interlude I:

Telliamed by Benoît de Maillet
Erewhon by Samuel Butler
Grimus by Salman Rushdie
Rocket Boys by Homer Hickam Jr
Holy Tango of Literature by Francis Heaney

THE above titles have something in common. They attempt to conceal rather than to reveal, to obscure rather than to illuminate. They are all anagrammatic.

The earliest example comes from Benoît de Maillet (1656-1738), a French nobleman, diplomat, natural historian and freethinker. It was his remarkable contention that life had originated in the oceans, and that the earth was over two billion years old. In the early eighteenth century these ideas were very unusual, antedating the founding of modern geology by at least fifty years. The problem was, essentially, seashells: shells in sedimentary rocks on the tops of mountains required some explanation, and de Maillet's was that the seas had originally been higher than the highest mountains, and had gradually lowered. This heretical opinion he put into the mouth, for safety, of the fictional Indian philosopher, Telliamed – whose name, it will be seen, is an anagram of his own name, de Maillet – in his major expository work *Telliamed, or Conversations between an Indian Philosopher and a French Missionary on the Diminution of the Sea*. In fact *Telliamed* is not strictly just an anagrammatic, but a palindromic book title.

A rather more familiar anagrammatic title is Samuel Butler's utopian satire *Erewhon* (1872). The land it described, with its Musical Banks and Hospitals for Incurable Bores, takes its name, as is well known, from a reversal of 'Nowhere'. However, *Erewhon* is not quite a perfect reversal: properly reversed, 'Nowhere' would be 'Erehwon'. Why did Butler leave the central 'wh' unreversed? The answer may lie in the fact that the book emerged from Butler's experiences in New Zealand in the early 1860s. For about four years he worked as a sheep farmer, and indeed one of the farms near where he worked, at the head of the Rangitata River in Canterbury, is today named 'Erewhon Station' in his honour. *Erewhon* drew extensively on New Zealand life, and particularly on Maori names, such as 'Kahabuka' and 'Mahaina' (both characters in the book). The name 'Erewhon' fits the Maori template. By leaving unreversed the central 'wh', Butler echoed Maori place-names such as Arowhena (North Island; a name also given to Mr Nosnibor's daughter) and Arowhenua (South Island, near Temuka). It seems likely then that the imperfect reversal was intended to add one more level of specifically New Zealand-inspired satire.

Grimus (1975) was Salman Rushdie's first novel, and, even judged by his later work, is remarkably obscure and complex. The plot follows the fortunes of one 'Flapping Eagle', who discovers an elixir of life that enables him to wander the earth looking for his sister, until finally he reaches Calf Island, a place on the other side of reality (sometimes on the other side of literature) ruled by the sinister figure of Grimus. The book is full of learned references to Islamic, Hindu, Greek, Roman, Christian and Norse myth and philosophy, and fell resoundingly flat with the critics. Among the book's strategies, anagrams are prominent: the novel's characters include the Gorfs, who live on the planet Thera in the galaxy of Yawy Klim (the Frogs who live on the planet Earth in the Milky Way), and the figure who gives the book its title, Grimus, has a name which is an anagram of Simurg, the mythical bird of Persian mysticism. Indeed the whole book can be understood as a re-writing of the twelfth-century Sufi poem *The Conference of the Birds* by Farid ud-Din Attar, which also deals with a quest for the Simurg. The title, then, announces the book's difficulty, a two-fingers-up to the reader before anyone even opens it. Perhaps it is significant that it is a first novel. Rushdie may have wanted to reject his readers before they rejected him.

Rocket Boys (1998), by Homer Hickam Jr, is an anagram of 'October Sky', and *October Sky* was the name of the film based on the book; *Rocket Boys* was subsequently re-published as *October Sky* to tie in with the film, and the book rose to number one on the *New York*

Times best-seller list. The book deals with the author's childhood in the 1950s in a mining-town in West Virginia, a place dedicated solely to 'extracting the millions of tons of rich bituminous coal that lay beneath it'. He and his friends are expected to follow their fathers and uncles into the industry, but instead (in a US version of a DH Lawrence novel) he becomes part of a group of rebel space-enthusiasts, the rocket boys. At the end of the film the two variants of the anagram are thematically fused: as the Rocket Boys let loose their most powerful rocket, the camera moves from the launch-pad to the townsfolk, their faces turned up to the sky in wonder, and the scene is intercut with footage from the launch of the Space Shuttle. And in fact Hickam did shrug off the surly bonds of earth himself, becoming an engineer for NASA and working on most of the major projects of twentieth-century spaceflight.

Francis Heaney's *Holy Tango of Literature* (2004) is perhaps the *ne plus ultra* of the anagrammatic title phenomenon. 'Holy Tango' unscrambles to 'Anthology', and each piece in the anthology is a parody of a writer based on an anagrammatic rendering of that writer's name. So we have 'Is a Sperm Like a Whale?' by William Shakespeare, 'A Wee Bladder' by Edward Albee, 'Errol Flynn's Not Dead' by Alfred Lord Tennyson and 'Bake Me Cutlets' by Samuel Beckett. Among the funniest is 'Kong Ran My Dealership' by Gerard Manley Hopkins:

Kong Ran My Dealership

TO OUR SALES LEADER

I hired last summer someone simian, King
    Kong of Indies islands, fifty-foot-fierce Gorilla, out of hiding
    After falling, feigning final death but breathing yet, and biding
Time there, how he swore that he could sell any third-rate thing
In a car lot! To the old, old Ford with a ding,
    As a snake oil sales spiel hooks a hill-hick, the ape was guiding
    A mark by monstrous hand, the rube then riding
Afar in that car, – to escape him, an appeasement on the wing!

Brute blarney to offer as options wheels, brakes, boot, seat
    Buckles, AND to roar. He breaks from his pen, he lumbers
Towards pale patrons, so dangerous, O who will he eat?

    No wonder of it: sheer fear makes Kong's sales numbers
Rise, though swift syringe stuck in his feet
    Can tranquilize, so King Kong slumbers.

14

Alice's Adventures in Wonderland (1865)
Through the Looking Glass and What Alice Found There (1871)
Lewis Carroll

BOTH of these famous titles contain the name 'Alice', and it is tempting to think that the second 'Alice' is the same as the first. Both are trusting, intelligent, curious, rather humourless little girls with a talent for getting into fantastic scrapes. In one sense they are the same; in another they are different.

To explain why, it is necessary to know a little about the author, Charles Lutwidge Dodgson, aka Lewis Carroll.[16] Dodgson was an Anglican deacon and fellow of Christ Church College, Oxford, the scion of a family of clergymen, and a lifelong bachelor who published several books on mathematics.[17] The popular image of him

---

16 'Lewis Carroll', a pseudonym, grew out of his real name, Charles Lutwidge Dodgson, since the Anglicized version of the German name 'Ludwig/Lutwidge' is 'Lewis', and the Latin for Charles is 'Carolus'.

17 There is a famous story that Queen Victoria was so taken with *Alice's Adventures in Wonderland* that she requested that Mr Carroll's next book be sent to her, and was disappointed when it arrived bearing the title *The Condensation of Determinants* – a story which, as Dodgson himself pointed out, was entirely untrue. In the foreword of his *Symbolic Logic* of 1896 he said it was 'utterly false in every particular'.

as a reclusive, stuttering, ivory-tower-dwelling academic is somewhat misleading. Even before the publication of the 'Alice' books his social contacts were wide-ranging: while still in his early twenties he made the personal acquaintance of John Ruskin, Alfred Tennyson, Ellen Terry and various other luminaries of the artistic, literary and theatrical worlds. He was an inveterate party-goer and entertainer, with a talent for mimicry and conjuring tricks. He was also a prolific pioneer photographer, specializing in portraits. His interest in photography overlapped to a great extent with his third main interest in life: prepubertal girls. He struck up dozens, perhaps hundreds of relationships with young girls, usually on holiday, photographed them, and kept up enormous correspondences with them. The roll-call of his conquests would fill pages: among them were Katie Brine, Agnes Grace, Madeleine Catherine Parnell, Xie Kitchin, Amy Hughes, Dymphna Ellis, Alice Constance Westmacott, Irene Macdonald, Zoe Strong and Gertrude Chataway, to name but a few. He was not a surreptitious snapper, in the manner of the prowling beach-photographer of modern nightmare, but always sought and obtained the permission and attendance of the parents. He often photographed his girls in costume – as beggar-girls, Red Riding Hoods, Chinamen – and made numerous nude studies. It was thought until fairly recently that none of these nudes had survived (he instructed his executors that they be destroyed), but a series of six Dodgson plates featuring little naked maidens was discovered in the Rosenbach collection in the 1970s.

To twenty-first century minds this all appears highly questionable. Many modern commentators have assumed that Dodgson was a paedophile. But a vogue for little girls in various states of undress was part of mainstream late-Victorian culture, much as the *putto* was a standard and unremarkable motif of the art of the baroque. Many other photographers specialized in just the same subjects, and photographs of naked girls routinely appeared on Christmas cards.

It has been assumed that among this extensive parade, Alice was special. She was certainly one of his earliest 'child-friends', though she was not the very earliest.[18] Her full name was Alice Liddell, the daughter of the Dean of Christ Church, Dr Henry Liddell. She was the middle child of a trio of charming sisters, Edith, Alice and Lorina, who at the time of meeting Dodgson on April 25, 1856 were two, three and six years old respectively. He first photographed them on June 3 of that year. The collodion wet-plate photography of the 1850s required long exposure times, and Dodgson was adept at persuading his young sitters to keep still: 'When we were thoroughly happy and amused at his stories,' Alice wrote in later life, 'he used to pose us, and expose the plates, before the right mood had passed. He seemed to have an endless fund of fantastical stories, which he made up as he told them...' The twenty-four-year-old Dodgson became a close friend of the family, attending teas and birthday parties, and soon began to take the sisters

---

18 He had formed friendships with little girls since early manhood. 'Boys are not in my line,' he wrote to a friend in February 1882. 'I think they are a mistake: girls are less objectionable.' Contrast the approach of JM Barrie (see chapter 20).

out on little trips, often telling them further extemporized stories. And on one summer's day – on a boat-trip on the Isis – he told them the story which became *Alice's Adventures in Wonderland*. It was July 4, 1862, and Edith, Alice and Lorina were eight, ten and thirteen years old. Robinson Duckworth, a friend of Dodgson's who accompanied them, later wrote: 'I rowed *stroke* and he rowed *bow* in the famous Long Vacation voyage to Godstow, when the three Miss Liddells were our passengers, and the story was actually composed and spoken over my shoulder for the benefit of Alice Liddell, who was acting as "cox" of our gig. I remember turning round and saying, "Dodgson, is this an extempore romance of yours?" And he replied, "Yes, I'm inventing as we go along."' Duckworth recalled that when they returned Alice asked Dodgson if he would write the story down, and he agreed, later staying up all night to commit to paper 'the recollections of the drolleries with which he had enlivened the afternoon'.

The title of the original hand-lettered book was *Alice's Adventures Under Ground*. Dodgson illustrated the book himself, and presented it to Alice in November 1864. But by this time he was barely on speaking terms with Alice and her family: relations with the Liddells had suffered a mysterious rupture. One guess is that Dodgson offered Lorina – or Alice – his hand in marriage, and the offer was not well received by the Liddells. The girls were still very young, of course, but possibly of greater importance was that they were the daughters of the Dean of Christ Church. Alice's mother was a social climber, and Dodgson was not a very good prospect.

Still, *Alice's Adventures Under Ground* was the fruit of those golden days on the Isis: and it was so well liked by the friends Dodgson showed it to that he determined to have it properly published, with proper illustrations. He decided on John Tenniel as the illustrator, thus bringing into being the one of most famous marriages of author and illustrator in the history of literature. However, Dodgson worried that the title *Alice's Adventures Under Ground* might be a little too prosaic for the published version (he even joked that readers might guess it had something to do with mining), and accordingly wrote on June 10, 1864 to a friend, Tom Taylor[19], for advice. He enclosed several titular possibilities in his letter, including *Alice Among the Elves*, *Alice Among the Goblins*, *Alice's Hour in Elfland*, *Alice's Hour in Wonderland*, and *Alice's Adventures in Wonderland*. Taylor seems to have picked the latter, and Dodgson concurred. Of the possibilities, it stands out as the superior choice, but in rather a poor field. The original title – *Alice's Adventures Under Ground* – is easily better, with its mythic connotations and its modern sense of a parallel social reality. *Alice's Adventures in Wonderland* was published in June 1865, became a best-seller, and has never been out of print.

So this was one Alice. It is less well known that the heroine of *Through the Looking-Glass and What Alice Found There* drew on a different Alice. This was the five-year-old Alice Theodora Raikes, Dodgson's distant cousin, who he first met in 1867. Writing much later in *The Times* in 1922, Alice told the story:

---

19 Taylor was the editor of *Punch* and a minor member of the Victorian literati. He had one other claim to fame: he was the author of a play called *Our American Cousin*. This was the play being performed when Lincoln was assassinated in 1865.

As children, we lived in Onslow Square and used to play in the garden behind the houses. Charles Dodgson used to stay with an old uncle there, and walk up and down, his hands behind him, on the strip of lawn. One day, hearing my name, he called me to him saying, 'So you are another Alice. I'm very fond of Alices. Would you like to come and see something which is rather puzzling?' We followed him into his house which opened, as ours did, upon the garden, into a room full of furniture with a tall mirror standing across one corner.

'Now,' he said, giving me an orange, 'first tell me which hand the little girl you see there has got it in.' After some perplexed contemplation, I said, 'The left hand.' 'Exactly,' he said, 'and how do you explain that?' I couldn't explain it, but seeing that some solution was expected, I ventured, 'If I was on the *other* side of the glass, wouldn't the orange still be in my right hand?' I can remember his laugh. 'Well done, little Alice,' he said. 'The best answer I've had yet.'

I heard no more then, but in after years was told that he said that had given him his first idea for *Through The Looking Glass,* a copy of which, together with each of his other books, he regularly sent me.

Derek Hudson, Dodgson's biographer, calls this 'the most important single inspiration for *Through the Looking-Glass*'.[20] It suggests that the first Alice is different from the second; or rather that neither the first Alice nor the second are crucially related to any living little girl. The Alices

20 The working title was *Behind the Looking-Glass, and What Alice Saw There*: it was later changed to *Through the Looking-Glass and What Alice Found There.*

were instead inspired by an amalgam of 'child-friends' Dodgson had built up during the course of his life, and we are incorrect if we think of either the Alice of the first book or the Alice of the second book as 'being' Alice Liddell, or, indeed, Alice Raikes. And when pressed on the matter later in life, Dodgson repeatedly denied that Alice was based on any real child. In a letter to Mary E Manners of December 5, 1885, for example, he said: 'thanks for the very sweet verses you have written about my dream-child (named after a real Alice, but none the less a dream-child) and her Wonderland.' This seems a little heartless, but given his extensive contact with little girls, it is intuitively convincing. Alice was essentially a fictional character, as Peter Pan was, or Winnie-the-Pooh – or Oliver Twist or the Woman in White.

15

The Pirates of Penzance (1879)
WS Gilbert and Arthur Sullivan

THE title of Gilbert and Sullivan's fifth operetta is more complex than it might at first appear.

On the surface it seems to indicate a fairly straightforward piece of Gilbertian topsy-turvydom. The 'pirates' of the title are all soft-hearted fellows, and their depredations are confined to Penzance, a seaside town in Cornwall rather a long way from the Spanish Main. The plot deals with a young man who is released from twenty-one years of piratical servitude only to discover that, due to the fact that he was born on February 29 in a leap year, he must spend a further sixty-three years with them. There is a love interest, of course, and a number of rousing choruses, the best-known of which is 'I am the very model of a modern Major-General' (the tune of which was taken by Tom Lehrer for his 'Elements Song'). However, the title conceals a joke. And the joke is all tied up with Gilbert and Sullivan's immediately preceding production, *HMS Pinafore*.

HMS Pinafore, or The Lass that Loved a Sailor[21] was the most successful of Gilbert and Sullivan's works up to that point, and launched them on a course that would produce their great mid-period successes: *The Pirates of Penzance, Patience, Iolanthe, The Mikado* and *Ruddigore*. It opened in London on May 25, 1878, and, despite a shaky start (the summer of 1878 was very hot and audiences stayed away from stuffy theatres) went on to run for 571 performances. An even greater success awaited it on the other side of the Atlantic. Only a few months after the first London performance, *Pinafore* played to enthusiastic audiences in Boston. The only problem was that this Boston production was nothing to do with either Gilbert or Sullivan. It was an unlicensed, 'pirate' performance that paid no fee to the authors.

In the 1870s there was no copyright agreement between the USA and Britain, and transatlantic imitators were free to do as they liked with any successful British stage production. *Pinafore* was an obvious target, and there were a dozen separate productions of it in Boston alone during 1878-9, including one for children with a libretto by Louisa May Alcott, and another set to music by John Philip Sousa. One US newspaper reported in 1879: 'At present, there are forty-two companies playing *Pinafore* about the country. Companies formed after 6pm yesterday are not included.'

---

21 *Pinafore* is a satire with strange origins. It was directed against WH Smith. William Henry Smith, the newsagent, magnate and politician, was appointed in 1877 as First Lord of the Admiralty, despite having no naval experience, and this rank appointeeism was Gilbert and Sullivan's target. The operetta was originally entitled *HMS Semaphore*, an appellation, as Gilbert admitted in an interview in *The World* in 1880, 'suggested entirely by rhyme... something had to rhyme with three cheers more'; but 'Semaphore' was not particularly funny, and was changed to 'Pinafore' at Sullivan's suggestion.

In fact the total ran to something like 150. There were all-black *Pinafores*, Yiddish *Pinafores*, German *Pinafores*, al fresco *Pinafores* set on ships; selections from *Pinafore* were heard from barrel organs and brass bands; there were *Pinafore* dolls, playing cards, clothing and tableware. Pirated librettos, scores and arrangements proliferated madly. The *New York Herald* called it 'the greatest craze – or lunacy'; others dubbed it '*Pinafore*-mania'. *Pinafore*'s catchphrases became a scourge.[22] Finally Gilbert, Sullivan and their business partner, Richard D'Oyly Carte, decided to mount a counter-attack and take an authentic *Pinafore* to the USA. It opened on December 1, 1879 at the Fifth Avenue Theater, New York, seven months after it had opened in London. But it fell flat. Everyone had seen it. The *Pinafore* craze was over.

Gilbert and Sullivan realized that if they were to seize some of the huge sums made by the American pirates, they would have to take a different tack. A bold plan was conceived. Their sixth operetta would open in the USA instead of Britain. Copyright would be established in Britain by a single performance the day before the US premiere. The US market would then be triumphantly milked, and the production would be brought home to Britain.

It was executed in the utmost secrecy. The first performance was staged at the Bijou Theatre, Paignton, Devon, on December 30, 1879, with a cast culled from a nearby touring production of *HMS Pinafore*. The cast were not rehearsed,

---

22 One involved the following piece of repartee: 'Never!' 'What, never?' 'Well, hardly ever.' This became so popular that the editor of one US newspaper complained that it had been used dozens of times in one edition of his paper alone. 'Never let me see it again,' he commanded his minions. 'What, never?' one of them asked. 'Well, hardly ever,' he found himself replying.

and wore their *Pinafore* costumes, with small alterations, while they read from sheet music. Nothing was published, and the sheet music was kept in hand-copied manuscript form; any potential pirates would have to listen attentively and write it all out by memory. Then, on December 31, *The Pirates of Penzance* opened at the Fifth Avenue Theater, New York, to a rapturous reception. Three separate and concurrent official productions were also mounted to satisfy what was anticipated (correctly) to be a *'Pirate*-mania'. Two of these were touring companies that visited Philadelphia, Boston, Chicago, Baltimore, New Orleans, St Louis and other cities. Gilbert and Sullivan then returned home to prepare for the London opening, which took place at the Opera Comique on April 3, again to an enthusiastic reception. It ran for a further 363 performances and has hardly been absent from the British stage since.

The pirates had been at least temporarily defeated. But in addition to the four 'official' productions, dozens of others sprang up to cash in. Nor were the sheet-music pirates deterred for long. By 1880 hundreds were offering piano, chamber and other arrangements, many not very accurate. Ultimately Gilbert and Sullivan failed to control American piracy, even if after *Pinafore* they had a much closer eye on the US market. (In 1882, for example, D'Oyly Carte sent Oscar Wilde on a lecture tour specifically designed to familiarize audiences with the Aesthetic movement in order to create a market for *Patience*, a parody of Aestheticism).

As a title, then, *The Pirates of Penzance* is a joke on two levels: Gilbert and Sullivan were mocking gentlemanly

Victorian English virtues, but were also taking a swipe at the copyright buccaneers who were pilfering their revenues. Of this second level there is no hint in the operetta itself.

Or perhaps there is. A buried reference to it may lurk in the famous Major-General's song. At one point he sings:

> I can tell undoubted Raphaels from Gerard Dows and
>   Zoffanies,
> I know the croaking chorus from The Frogs of
>   Aristophanes!
> Then I can hum a fugue of which I've heard the music's
>   din afore,
> And whistle all the airs from that infernal nonsense
>   Pinafore!

Being able to hum a tune of which you've 'heard the music's din afore' might be an essential skill for a pirate.

16

Treasure Island (1883)
Robert Louis Stevenson

TREASURE Island was Robert Louis Stevenson's first book, and is the book he remains best-known for. George Moore[23] was very unkind on this point, saying that Stevenson could not have been much of a writer:

> I will state frankly that Mr. R.L. Stevenson never wrote a line that failed to delight me; but he never wrote a book. You arrive at a strangely just estimate of a writer's worth by the mere question: 'What is he the author of?', for every writer whose work is destined to live is the author of one book that outshines the other, and, in popular imagination, epitomises his talent and position. What is Shakespeare the author of? What is Milton the author of? What is Fielding the author of? What is Byron the author of? What is Carlyle the author of? What is Thackeray the author of? What is Zola the author of? What is Mr.

---

23 George Moore, the prolific, now little-read, Irish novelist and dramatist. Ford Madox Ford said of Moore: 'I have never met a critic with any pretensions to knowledge of letters who would not acknowledge when challenged that Moore was infinitely the most skilful man of letters of his day. The most skilful in the whole world...Yet in an infinite number of reviews and *comptes rendus* of the literature of the world that I have read – and written – George Moore is almost invariably forgotten. That is due perhaps to the fact that he belonged to no school in England; perhaps to his want of personal geniality, perhaps to something more subtle.'

> Swinburne the author of? Mr. Stevenson is the author of
> shall I say, 'Treasure Island', or what?

Nevertheless this book, slight though it may be, was crucial to Stevenson. Without *Treasure Island* it seems unlikely that he would have written anything else at all: he produced it at the nadir of his professional ambition.

Its composition came about as the result of a sort of synaesthesia.

By the age of 31 Stevenson had made many attempts at writing a novel, but to his despair each attempt had 'stopped inexorably like a schoolboy's watch'. His attempts had included tales such as 'Rathillet', 'The Pentland Rising', 'The King's Pardon' (otherwise 'Park Whitehead'), 'Edward Daven', 'A Country Dance', and 'A Vendetta in the West', but all of these had struggled only to the length of a short story or novella before petering out; and although a few short stories and articles had found publishers, the main event, a novel, seemed beyond his powers. He had never earned a living, despite being a married man: 'I passed my days in toil, the futility of which would sometimes make my cheek to burn,' he wrote. 'I was the head of a family; I had lost my health; I had never yet paid my way, never yet made £200 a year.'

Then in 1881, in Kinnaird, near Pitlochry, he found himself house-bound by rainy weather, and to pass the time joined his young stepson, Lloyd Osbourne, in painting pictures. Stevenson wrote:

On one of these occasions, I made the map of an island;
it was elaborately and (I thought) beautifully coloured;
the shape of it took my fancy beyond expression; it contained harbours that pleased me like sonnets; and with
the unconsciousness of the predestined, I ticketed my
performance 'Treasure Island'. I am told there are people
who do not care for maps, and find it hard to believe.
The names, the shapes of the woodlands, the courses
of the roads and rivers, the prehistoric footsteps of man
still distinctly traceable up hill and down dale, the mills
and the ruins, the ponds and the ferries, perhaps the
STANDING STONE or the DRUIDIC CIRCLE on the
heath; here is an inexhaustible fund of interest for any
man with eyes to see or twopence-worth of imagination
to understand with! No child but must remember laying
his head in the grass, staring into the infinitesimal forest
and seeing it grow populous with fairy armies.
Somewhat in this way, as I paused upon my map of
'Treasure Island', the future character of the book began
to appear there visibly among imaginary woods; and
their brown faces and bright weapons peeped out upon
me from unexpected quarters, as they passed to and
fro, fighting and hunting treasure, on these few square
inches of a flat projection. The next thing I knew I had
some papers before me and was writing out a list of
chapters.

With the visual stimulus of the map Stevenson had at
last found fluency. He worked in the mornings, and after
lunch, read the chapters aloud to his family. His father was
particularly taken with the results, and began to collaborate,

preparing an inventory of Billy Bones' chest, and contrib-
uting the name of Flint's old ship, the *Walrus*. As if by
magic, a publisher turned up through the agency of one
Dr Alexander Japp, a family friend, who listened enthusiastically to the readings, then carried off the manuscript in
his briefcase. It was published in instalments in 1881-82 in
the magazine *Young Folks*, and here, but for the publisher's
intervention, literary history might have been different.
Stevenson's original title was *The Sea-Cook*, but the publisher changed it to *Treasure Island*, closer to the fount of
inspiration. *The Sea-Cook* was in reference to Long John
Silver, ex-chef of the *Walrus*; the new title, *Treasure Island*
cut to the heart of the matter, and depended, once again,
crucially on the map.

The serialization was not a particular success – that
would only come when it appeared as a novel in 1883 – but
Stevenson felt a weight had been lifted from his shoul-
ders. He had written 'The End' under a lengthy work of
fiction, and had had it published. He dedicated it to Lloyd
Osbourne, the boy drawing pictures:

> *To* LLOYD OSBOURNE
> An American Gentleman
> In accordance with whose classic taste
> The following narrative has been designed
> It is now, in return for numerous delightful hours
> And with the kindest wishes, dedicated
> By his affectionate friend
> *THE AUTHOR.*

Stevenson later wrote: 'I have said the map was the most of the plot. I might almost say it was the whole.' He had good reason, since the very map Stevenson had drawn that rainy afternoon was the one Jim Hawkins found among Billy Bones' possessions at the Admiral Benbow Inn, and which led him to set sail in the *Hispaniola*. Without the map, there would be no 'X marks the spot', which was purely an artifact of the map, nor any of the salty romance of be-parroted pirates and cheese-craving castaways. The map pointed the way to the treasure Jim was able to find, the treasure of the book Stevenson was able to write, and the treasure of the career he was able to grasp.

17

The Importance of Being Earnest (1895)
Oscar Wilde

THE Importance of Being Earnest contains a pun: that much seems clear. George Bernard Shaw said in his review of the play in 1895 that the wordplay on Ernest/Earnest was not in fact a very good pun, and that the title as a whole was rather laboured and old-fashioned:

> It is somewhat surprising to find Mr Oscar Wilde, who does not usually model himself on Mr Henry Arthur Jones, giving his latest play a five-chambered title like *The Case of Rebellious Susan*. So I suggest with some confidence that *The Importance of Being Earnest* dates from a period long anterior to Susan. [...] the punning title and several of the more farcical passages recall the epoch of the late H.J. Byron.

But Shaw might have missed something. 'Earnest' is certainly a pun, but quite likely a double pun. As well as playing on the name 'Ernest' it may also play on *Urning*, the German word for 'homosexual' coined in the 1860s by the sexologist Karl Heinrich Ulrichs. The evidence for the link between 'earnest' and *Urning* is suggestive rather than conclusive, but, as suggestive evidence goes, it might be considered 'highly suggestive'.

Karl Heinrich Ulrichs (1825-1895) was a German jurist, sex researcher, polymath and awkward customer, a contender for the title of the first 'out' gay man in the modern era, and the author of a series of works exploring what he called 'the riddle of man-manly love'. In the nineteenth century homosexual acts were criminal in Germany and throughout Europe, and Ulrichs was taking significant risks. His approach to the problem was to argue that homosexuality should be taken out of the criminal sphere and introduced into the spheres of medicine, psychology and biology; he was a major influence on later thinkers such as Krafft-Ebing and Freud. His now-bizarre-sounding terminology of sexual types (including categories such as *Urning, Urningin* and *Dioning*) was in use among sexologists and the educated public until the 1920s, both in Germany and abroad. This was an era, it must be remembered, in which the word 'homosexual' was also new, and not yet universally adopted: it had only been invented in 1869 by the Hungarian-German writer Karl-Maria Kertbeny. Wilde would have heard of the word *Urning* and certainly used its English equivalent, 'Uranian'.[24] For example, in a letter of 1898, Wilde wrote:

> A patriot put in prison for loving his country loves his
> country, and a poet put in prison for loving boys loves
> boys. To have altered my life would have been to have

---

24 'Uranian' was common for male homosexuals, in reference to the god Uranus, who had given birth to Aphrodite without intervention from any woman. *Urning* was similarly derived.

> admitted that Uranian love is ignoble. I hold it to be
> noble – more noble than other forms.

The punning relation between *Urning*, Uranian and Ernest/Earnest is difficult to prove, but it seems to have been present in at least one important source: the title of a collection of homoerotic love lyrics published three years before Wilde's play, *Love in Earnest* (1892), by John Gambril Nicholson, a prominent 'Uranian' poet and homosexual advocate of the 1880s and 1890s. One poem in the collection, 'Of Boys' Names', champions Ernest as the loveliest name of them all, and it is tempting to think that this was for punning reasons. Here is the poem in full:

Of Boys' Names

Old memories of the Table Round
In Percival and Lancelot dwell,
Clement and Bernard bring the sound
Of anthems in the cloister-cell,

And Leonard vies with Lionel
In stately step and kingly frame,
And Kenneth speaks of field and fell,
And Ernest sets my heart a-flame.

One name can make my pulses bound,
No peer it owns, nor parallel,
By it is Vivian's sweetness drowned,
And Roland, full as organ-swell;

Though Frank may ring like silver bell,
And Cecil softer music claim,
They cannot work the miracle, —
'Tis Ernest sets my heart a-flame.

Cyril is lordly, Stephen crowned
With deathless wreaths of asphodel,
Oliver whispers peace profound,
Herbert takes arms his foes to quell,

Eustace with sheaves is laden well,
Christopher has a nobler fame,
And Michael storms the gates of Hell,
But Ernest sets my heart a-flame.

Envoy:
My little Prince, Love's mystic spell
Lights all the letters of your name,
And you, if no one else, can tell
Why Ernest sets my heart a-flame.

Nicholson and Wilde appeared together in an issue of *The Chameleon* magazine of 1894, a periodical mentioned during Wilde's trials. If Wilde did not know Nicholson personally, he must certainly have known of him.

There are a couple of other lines of evidence suggesting that 'Earnest/Ernest' was intended to mean 'homosexual' in Wilde's play. The first is that *The Importance of Being Earnest* is, in any case, an encoded text. The most obvious piece of encoding is in the word 'Bunbury', with its verbal form 'Bunburying'. Ostensibly, 'Bunburying' has no especial homosexual meaning. Algernon explains that he has invented an invaluable permanent invalid called Bunbury, in order that he can go down into the country whenever he chooses. But 'Bunbury' surely also suggests illicit homosexual activity. Consider the way Algernon goes on, explicitly contrasting the pleasures of 'Bunbury' with the duties of marriage:

> ALGERNON. Nothing will induce me to part with Bunbury, and if you ever get married, which seems to me extremely problematic, you will be very glad to know Bunbury. A man who marries without knowing Bunbury has a very tedious time of it.
> JACK. That is nonsense. If I marry a charming girl like Gwendolen, and she is the only girl I ever saw in my life that I would marry, I certainly won't want to know Bunbury.

Algernon, in fact, has 'Bunburyed all over Shropshire,' a line that must surely have provoked gales of laughter among the green-carnationed contingent of Wilde's audience. And as with Bunbury, so surely with Ernest. Ernest symbolizes the double life: he is Ernest in town and Jack in the country. The double life is of course a major theme of Wilde's – most notably in *The Picture of Dorian Gray* – and had its obvious homosexual resonances in the era of the Criminal Law Amendment Act, which required gay men to lead a double life or face prosecution and imprisonment. As the critic Christopher Craft puts it:

> While mimicking the dramatic conventions of heterosexual triumph, [Wilde] inserted within them the

legally unspeakable traces of homosexual delight: inscribed them, no less, where perhaps they would be least expected and certainly most disruptive – into the vocables of the paternal signifier, itself the guarantor of heterophallic order. The Urning would hide in 'Earnest' – thereby punburying and Bunburying at the same time.

And if this does not convince, consider Gwendolen's remark on Ernest's name: 'It is a divine name. It has a music of its own. It produces vibrations.' A remarkably similar sentiment to that in John Gambril Nicholson's poem, is it not?

Though Frank may ring like silver bell,
And Cecil softer music claim,
They cannot work the miracle,–
'Tis Ernest sets my heart a-flame.

18

Three Sisters (1900)
Anton Chekhov

THE three sisters of Chekhov's title live in a provincial backwater. Olga, the eldest, is a schoolteacher, as yet unmarried, who feels 'like an old woman' (she's 28), but is nevertheless full of longing for adventure and gaiety. Masha, the middle sister, is married to a dull schoolteacher and also feels trapped. Irina, the youngest, is obsessed with the idea of working and benefiting humanity, envying the lot of 'a labourer who gets up at the crack of dawn and breaks stones in the street'. The sisters are all Moscow-born, and desire fiercely to return to the capital, the locus of everything exciting, modern and free: the refrain of the play is 'To Moscow! To Moscow!' When a garrison is stationed in the town, and a group of cultured officers attach themselves to the sisters, the effect is galvanic. Olga realizes that her teaching career is a waste of time and considers leaving the school; Masha has an affair with one of the officers; and Irina receives a proposal from one Baron Tusenbach, who is later killed in a duel. This death, which a different dramatist would surely have made a great deal of, happens off-stage, almost casually; there are no real events in the play, and the action is philosophical rather than actual. We hear a succession of conversations about the meaning of life and death, the future of humanity, the passing of time and the importance of Moscow, sprinkled with statements about birch trees and the settling of snow; and when the soldiers are inevitably moved on, the sisters are left bereft, still wondering what it all means, and still as far away from Moscow as ever. Olga tries to console her sisters in the last speech of the play as the soldiers march away:

> The music is so gay and cheerful, I do so want to live. Oh, dear! Time will pass and we shall be gone forever. We shall be forgotten, and people will no longer remember our faces and our voices. But our sufferings will turn into joy for those who live after us. There will be peace and happiness on earth, and we who live now will be remembered with gratitude and blessing. Oh, my dear sisters, our lives are not finished yet! We shall go on living! The music is so gay and cheerful. It seems that any minute now we shall find out why we are alive and why we are suffering. Oh, if only we knew! If only we knew!

The actors at the first rehearsals couldn't decide whether it was a comedy or a tragedy, and when the play opened on January 31, 1901, large swathes of the audience were baffled by the rambling speeches, the pauses, the lack of any events. But its fame grew rapidly, and even by Chekhov's death in 1904 *Three Sisters* was acclaimed as a landmark in world theatre. It was later enthusiastically claimed by the Soviets, especially for eerily prescient speeches such as Baron Tusenbach's in Act One:

> The time is coming when something huge will overwhelm
> us. A strong, healthy storm is on its way. It is already quite
> close and soon it will sweep away the idleness and com-
> placency in our society, the prejudice against work and the
> stagnant boredom. I shall work, and in another twenty-
> five or thirty years everyone will work. Everyone.

The title and theme were influenced by events that had happened more than a decade earlier.

Chekhov in the late 1880s was both successful and well-off, supporting a large extended family by his writing. But in May 1888, Moscow life and the demands of his dependents were beginning to grate, and he decided to escape to the country, renting a dacha at Luka in the Ukraine. He rhapsodized ironically to his friend Suvorin about its 'old, overgrown gardens, highly poetic and melancholy boarded-up manors where souls of beautiful women dwell, to say nothing of ancient moribund butlers, who look back fondly on their serf days, and of young ladies pining for the most stereotyped kind of love.' The owners were the Lintvaryov family, formerly wealthy but now existing in an atmosphere of genteel poverty. The head of the household was one Madame Lintvaryova, a politically-radical, Schopenhauer-reading defender of the arts, who immediately took to Chekhov. She had three daughters: the eldest was Zinaida, of whom Chekhov said:

> A doctor, she is the pride of the family, and the peasants
> say, a saint… She has a brain tumour; this has left her

completely blind, she has epilepsy and constant head-
aches. She knows what to expect, and talks about her
imminent death stoically with striking calm.

The middle daughter was Elena, also a doctor, though considered too plain for marriage, and the youngest Natalia,
later an intimate of the Chekhov circle, travelling with
Chekhov's sister and visiting Chekhov on numerous occasions at Yalta and Melikhovo. One son was under house
arrest for his radical politics.

Chekhov had a hugely enjoyable time at Luka, fishing,
flirting, bathing, boating, attending fairs, talking, talking,
talking (there was no television), though he was disconcerted by the lack of a brothel in the nearby town. He toyed
with the idea of buying an estate in the district to start a
writer's retreat, and continued to visit on and off throughout the rest of his life.

It is difficult not to see the three sisters of the play as rep-
resentations of the three Lintvaryov sisters, with Zinaida,
Elena and Natalia becoming Olga, Masha and Irina. And
he mined his experiences at Luka for all they were worth,
not just in *Three Sisters* but also in endless short stories of
imprisoned, unfulfilled women in boarded-up dachas.[25]

The sisters' constant longing for Moscow was sharply
at odds with Chekhov's own feelings at the time he was

25 There were no officers at the Lintvaryovs, but it is quite possible that Chekhov was thinking of an earlier experience, in 1883, when he had stayed at Voskresensk with his brother
Vania, and had been introduced to officers of a local battalion. Chekhov drew on this experience in his short story 'The Kiss', which, when it appeared in 1887 (shortly before his trip
to Luka), convinced many that Chekhov had himself been a serving officer in an artillery
regiment. His experience at Voskresensk, it seems, fused with his experience at Luka, the
garrison officers entering and disrupting the shuttered world of the sisters, and providing
the dramatic engine of the play.

staying at the Lintvaryovs. On a warm Ukrainian night in August 1888 he wrote:

> O, how hard it is for me to leave here! Especially now, with the river more beautiful every day, the weather magnificent, the peasants bringing in the hay... The thought of Moscow with its cold climate, bad plays, snack bars and Russian ideas makes my flesh creep. I wish I could spend the winters far, far away.

19

The Tale of Peter Rabbit (1902)
Beatrix Potter

IT will come as no surprise that Beatrix Potter had a pet
rabbit, nor even perhaps that his name was Peter. Perhaps
less widely known is that this creature has a very compre-
hensive biography. He was a Belgian buck hare (there was
a vogue in the 1890s for 'Belgian hares' but they were not
really hares, but rabbits), and his full name was Peter Piper.
He was, Beatrix wrote, 'bought at a very tender age, in the
Uxbridge Road, Shepherd's Bush, for the exorbitant sum of
4/6,' and his new owner soon made him work for his sup-
per. 'He really is good at tricks, when hungry, in private,
jumping (stick, hands, hoop, back and forward), ringing
little bell and drumming on a tambourine.' Unfortunately
he would never do the tricks in company. In her journal she
described a tea to which she had brought Peter: 'He caused
shrieks of amusement by sitting up in the arm-chair and
getting on to the tea-table. The children were satisfied, but
it is tiresome that he will never show off.'

Peter joined the immortals with a letter Beatrix wrote to
the sick child of her former governess. The letter, to the

five-year-old Noel Moore, was sent on September 4, 1893. 'I don't know what to write to you,' Beatrix said, 'so I shall tell you a story about four little rabbits whose names were – Flopsy, Mopsy, Cottontail, and Peter. They lived with their mother in a sand bank under the root of a big fir tree. "Now, my dears," said old Mrs. Bunny, "you may go into the field or down the lane, but don't go into Mr McGregor's garden..."'[26] The letter was illustrated with sixteen line-drawn vignettes of the adventures of Peter. Beatrix was a keen amateur artist, and the rabbits were rendered with a mastery of angle and movement. The next day, so as not to leave out Noel's younger brother Eric, Beatrix wrote another letter about 'a frog called Mr Jeremy Fisher'.

In 1900 Noel's mother suggested that the picture-letters might be made into books, and Beatrix borrowed the letters back to work on them. She chose the Peter Rabbit letter to start with, and made it into a book called 'The Tale of Peter Rabbit and Mr McGregor's Garden'. It was sent to several publishers but returned by all of them (including Frederick Warne and Co., its eventual publishers).[27] Beatrix, irritated by their havering replies, drew a series of sketches featuring 'Miss Potter and her publishers,' captioning them: 'The publisher is a gentleman who prints books, and he wants a bigger book than he has got enough money to pay for! and Miss Potter has arguments with him... I wonder if that

---

26 In September 1893 Beatrix happened to be on holiday at Eastwood, Perthshire, and Mr McGregor was the name of the man who had leased the house (and garden) to the Potter family.

27 Beatrix had some very successful competitors. In 1895 *The Adventures of Two Dutch Dolls and a Golliwogg* by Florence and Bertha Upton had sold copies in the tens of thousands, and in 1899 Helen Bannerman's *The Story of Little Black Sambo* (followed by its sequel, *The Story of Little Black Mingo*) appeared, also a nursery sensation.

book will ever be printed! I think Miss Potter will go off to another publisher soon!'

Finally Beatrix decided to self-publish. In September 1901 she ordered 250 copies of her book, now called *The Tale of Peter Rabbit*, from a London printer, at a cost of eleven pounds. They were ready just in time for Christmas, and proved very popular with friends and relatives. But just at this point Warne changed its mind and made Beatrix an offer.[28] As long as she would cut the book down and agree to illustrate it in colour throughout, they would bring out an edition of 8,000, with royalties at threepence a copy. Beatrix did agree, and the Warne edition was published in October 1902. It sold out immediately, necessitating a second edition – and then a third, fourth, and fifth. By Christmas 1902 – two months after it had first appeared – 28,000 had been printed. In November 1903 Beatrix wrote: 'The public must be fond of rabbits! what an appalling quantity of Peter.'

How to account for the success of this first book? How, in fact, to account for its current lifetime sales figures, in the tens of millions? *Peter Rabbit* was unusual in children's books of the time that it drew heavily on Beatrix's accurate observations of real rabbits – their postures in exploration, fear, sleep, flight and feeding. It was accompanied by gorgeous miniatures of the English countryside, culled from many years of experience as an amateur botanical illustrator. The story is rooted in nature, both in picture and text, which gives it its integrity, and yet these absolutely natural

---

28 In her correspondence Beatrix dealt chiefly with the younger son of the house, Norman Warne, who became her fiancé, but died of leukaemia before they could marry.

animals are shown talking, wearing clothes, eating from plates and going to bed. The human and animal worlds somehow overlay one another, each perfectly believable while being mutually contradictory. There is also real dramatic tension in *The Tale of Peter Rabbit*, as in other Potter books such as *The Tale of Pigling Bland* or *The Tale of Jemima Puddleduck*. If Peter, Pigling or Jemima are caught they will be killed, and readers are made quite aware of the fact. Perhaps also in Mr McGregor's garden there is a suggestion of Eden – a paradise which Peter tries to return to but is driven from by a Scotsman with a flaming hoe. There is a curious depth to *Peter Rabbit*.

The real Peter Rabbit, Peter Piper, lived to the age of nine, dying on January 26, 1901, a rather inconvenient date for Beatrix. She wrote to Warne's that Peter had expired 'just before I began the drawings and now when they are finished I have got another rabbit, and the drawings look wrong.' But she obviously missed him, and in an inscription to a copy of the book that bears his name, she wrote: 'Whatever the limitations of his intellect or outward shortcomings of his fur, and his ears and toes, his disposition was uniformly amiable and his temper unfailingly sweet. An affectionate and a quiet friend.'

In later years, however, as Peter-mania began to take a grip on the entire civilized globe, she found herself mildly outraged by the whole business: 'I believe my attitude of mind towards my own successful publications has been comical; at one time I almost loathed Peter Rabbit, I was so sick of him. I still cannot understand his perennial success.'

20

Peter Pan (1904)
JM Barrie

ON April 5, 1960, Peter Llewellyn Davies, a London publisher, entered Sloane Square tube station and threw himself under a train. When the papers realized who the corpse was, it was front-page news. 'PETER PAN'S DEATH LEAP'; 'THE TRAGEDY OF PETER PAN'; 'PETER PAN COMMITS SUICIDE'; 'THE BOY WHO NEVER GREW UP IS DEAD'. The *Daily Express* reported:

> Until he died at 68 Peter Davies was Peter Pan. He was the Little Boy Who Never Grew Up; the boy who believed in fairies. The name was the gift to him of play-wright Sir James Barrie and Peter Davies hated it all his life. But he was never allowed to forget it until, as a shy, retiring publisher, he fell to his death on Tuesday night.

It was a great story, but the truth wasn't quite so simple.

By 1897 JM Barrie had achieved considerable success on both sides of the Atlantic with works such as *Sentimental Tommy* (1896) and *The Little Minister* (1897). He was on personal terms with many of the great literary figures of the day, and could raise his eyebrows independently of one another and wiggle his ears, a talent which fascinated children. He first met Peter Llewellyn Davies in Kensington Park Gardens in 1897, though Peter at that point was not yet one year old: Barrie was drawn chiefly to his two brothers, George, aged five, and Jack, aged four. He soon became close to the family, and especially to the mother, Sylvia Llewellyn Davies, who turned out to have an impeccable literary pedigree: she was the daughter of the writer George du Maurier, author of the novels *Peter Ibbetson* and *Trilby*, the latter an enormous success in late Victorian Britain.[29] Peter Llewellyn Davies was in fact named after the hero of *Peter Ibbetson*.

The first stirrings of *Peter Pan* were in a novel of 1902, *The Little White Bird*, which is mainly about Barrie's close relationship with George. It tells the story of one Captain W – based on Barrie himself – who wants to have a son of his own, and achieves this vicariously by befriending a young and penurious couple (transparently the Llewellyn Davieses). In the book, Peter Pan is a baby that has flown away from his mother to live *al fresco* on an island in the Serpentine. The book explains that all babies exist originally as birds, but lose their power of flight when they are reborn as humans. Peter, however, by a quirk of fate, is still able to fly. When he tries to fly home he sees that his mother has a new baby:

---

[29] It is from *Trilby* (1894) that the name 'Svengali' originates. The novel also christened the hat. It made its author rich and famous for life, and on his early death in 1896 he was able to leave a substantial legacy for Sylvia. George du Maurier was the father of the actor Gerald du Maurier and the grandfather of Daphne du Maurier.

Peter called, 'Mother! mother!' but she heard him not; in vain he beat his little limbs against the iron bars. He had to fly back, sobbing, to the Gardens, and he never saw his dear again. What a glorious boy he had meant to be to her. Ah, Peter, we who have made the great mistake, how differently we should all act at the second chance. But Solomon was right; there is no second chance, not for most of us. When we reach the window it is Lock-out Time. The iron bars are up for life.

The Little White Bird did very well, and Barrie, an established playwright, saw its stage potential. He decided to develop the Peter Pan aspect in particular, drawing on the stories and games of pirates and castaways he and the Llewellyn Davies boys (there were eventually five: George, Jack, Peter, Michael and Nico) had invented in Kensington Park Gardens and elsewhere. The play was originally titled 'Peter and Wendy', then changed to 'The Great White Father', before Charles Frohman, Barrie's American producer, convinced Barrie to change it to *Peter Pan*. It opened at the Duke of York's Theatre, London, on December 27, 1904, and was an extremely ambitious production, requiring juveniles flying on wires, a crocodile, an eagle, a lion, a jaguar and a cast of several dozen. Barrie was nervous that it would prove a costly failure, but in the event it was the smash hit of the year. When the actress Nina Boucicault, as Peter Pan, asked the audience at the first performance: 'Do you believe in fairies? If you believe, wave your handkerchiefs and clap your hands!' the response was so deafening that she burst out crying. Daphne du Maurier wrote of her father Gerald, who appeared as Captain Hook: 'When Hook first paced his quarter-deck in the year of 1904, children were carried screaming from the stalls...'

Following the success of the play, the Peter Pan chapters from *The Little White Bird* were published separately as *Peter Pan in Kensington Gardens* in 1906, and novelized in 1911 under the title *Peter and Wendy.*[30]

The name 'Peter' thus came substantially from Peter Llewellyn Davies, the 'baby' of the family in 1897; but the character and myth of Peter Pan came from the games of the Llewellyn Davies boys and Barrie's inventions around them. Barrie wrote in 1928:

> I made Peter by rubbing the five of you violently
> together, as savages with two sticks produce a flame. I
> am sometimes asked who and what Peter is, but that is
> all he is, the spark I got from you.

The surname Pan was from the Greek godling of nature and misrule. *The Little White Bird* played particularly to this idea, portraying him riding on a goat:

> If you ask your mother whether she knew about Peter
> Pan when she was a little girl she will say, 'Why, of
> course, I did, child,' and if you ask her whether he rode
> on a goat in those days she will say, 'What a foolish
> question to ask; certainly he did.' [...] Of course, it also
> shows that Peter is ever so old, but he is really always
> the same age, so that does not matter in the least. His age

---

30 This later became simply *Peter Pan*. The name 'Wendy', which in 1904 was all but unknown, was coined by Margaret Henley (daughter of WE Henley), who died aged 6. She called Barrie 'My Friendy', which, because she could not pronounce her 'r's, became 'Wendy'.

is one week, and though he was born so long ago he has
never had a birthday, nor is there the slightest chance of
his ever having one.

Peter Llewellyn Davies, then, was sandwiched between
two well-known fictional creations – *Peter Ibbetson* and
Peter Pan, a burden for later life to rival Christopher Robin
Milne's or Alice Liddell's. He was teased continually at
Eton as 'the real Peter Pan,' and grew to hate any association with the book he called 'that terrible masterpiece'. He
wrote:

> What's in a name? My God, what isn't? If that perenni-
> ally juvenile lead, if that boy so fatally committed to an
> arrestation of his development, had only been dubbed
> George, or Jack, or Michael, or Nicholas, what miseries
> would have been spared me.

But worse was to come. In 1907 his father died of a sarcoma
of the jaw, followed by his mother in 1910, of cancer. Then
the First World War intervened. George, the eldest, was
killed in 1915, and Peter enlisted in 1916, aged nineteen, just
in time to serve in the battle of the Somme. He survived,
but Denis Mackail, Barrie's biographer, wrote of Peter:
'He has been through something more than a furnace, and
what was left of him was for a long while little more than a
ghost.' Then, in 1921, Michael, the fourth brother, drowned
while swimming. Peter had now suffered the deaths of
two parents and two brothers, had suffered a childhood
blighted by taunts, endured the horror of trench warfare

for two years, and was still only in his mid-twenties. It seems to be a combination of these traumas, as well as alcoholism, ill-health, and resentment at Barrie for not leaving him anything in his will[31], which led to his suicide in 1960, and not simply the fact, as the newspapers implied, that he could no longer stand being Peter Pan.

---

31 Peter's son Ruthven said that this made his father bitter, since he considered that 'he, Peter, was the inspiration for Peter Pan and therefore it was only reasonable that my father should inherit everything from Barrie on that basis.'

21

The Necronomicon (no date)
not by HP Lovecraft

HP Lovecraft was one of the early exponents of horror fantasy. He is best known for a series of short stories and novelettes – among them 'Nyarlathotep' (1920), 'The Nameless City' (1921) and 'The Call of Cthulhu' (1926) – that came collectively to be known as the 'Cthulhu Mythos'. The central premise of this Mythos is that a race of Great Old Ones, who once ruled the Earth, remain behind hidden from the eyes of men. 'The Call of Cthulhu' begins:

> We live on a placid island of ignorance in the midst
> of black seas of infinity, and it was not meant that we
> should voyage far. The sciences, each straining in its
> own direction, have hitherto harmed us little; but some
> day the piecing together of dissociated knowledge will
> open up such terrifying vistas of realty, and of our own
> frightful position therein, that we shall either go mad
> from the revelation or flee from the deadly light into the
> peace and safety of a new dark age.

In this deadly light are to be found Yuggoth, Great Cthulhu, Tsathoggua, Yog-Sothoth, R'lyeh, Nyarlathotep, Azathoth, Hastur, Klarkash-Ton, Bethmoora, L'mur-Kathulos, Bran and the Magnum Innominandum. Lovecraft delighted in this sort of fantastic nomenclature, deriving in part from the supernatural fiction of Lord Dunsany ('Bethmoora' is the title of a Dunsany short story) as well as, earlier, the horror fiction of Edgar Allan Poe. Some of these names were actually jokes – his 'Atlantean priest Klarkash-Ton' was named after a friend, Clark Ashton Smith, and Lovecraft sometimes referred to himself as 'Eich-Pi-El' ('HPL'). One of the stock properties of the Cthulhu Mythos was a *grimoire*, or book of spells, called the *Necronomicon*, for summoning entities from beyond the grave. It turns up for the first time in 'The Hound' (1924), when two grave-robbing friends find an amulet with a symbol of a winged dog:

> Immediately upon beholding this amulet we knew that
> we must possess it; that this treasure alone was our logi-
> cal pelf from the centuried grave. Even had its outlines
> been unfamiliar we would have desired it, but as we
> looked more closely we saw that it was not unfamiliar.
> Alien it indeed was to all art and literature which sane
> and balanced readers know, but we recognized it as
> the thing hinted of in the forbidden *Necronomicon* of the
> mad Arab Abdul Alhazred; the ghastly soul-symbol of
> the forbidden corpse-eating cult of inaccessible Leng, in
> central Asia.

The accursed *Necronomicon* was supposed to have real existence in the Miskatonic Library at Arkham, New England. In 'The Dunwich Horror' (1928) the eight-foot tall Wilbur Whately is a student of the book, and transcribes some of it, as follows:

> *Yog-Sothoth* knows the gate. *Yog-Sothoth* is the gate. *Yog-Sothoth* is the key and guardian of the gate. Past, present, future, all are one in *Yog-Sothoth*.

But this information does no good to Wilbur, who is attacked by a police dog that tears his clothes off. Underneath, Wilbur is a hideous hybrid monster, with legs like a dinosaur's, eyes on his hips, and 'long greenish-grey tentacles with red sucking mouths' emerging from his abdomen. When he dies he dissolves into a 'sticky whitish mass'.

In 1936 HPL waxed more specific in an essay called 'A History of the Necronomicon':

> Composed by Abdul Alhazred, a mad poet of Sanaa, in Yemen, who is said to have flourished during the period of the Ommiade Caliphs, circa AD. 700. [...] In his last years Alhazred dwelt in Damascus, where the *Necronomicon (Al Azif)* was written, and of his final death or disappearance (AD. 738) many terrible and conflicting things are told. He is said by Ebn Khallikan (twelfth century biographer) to have been seized by an invisible monster in broad daylight and devoured horribly before a large number of fright-frozen witnesses. Of his madness many things are told. He claimed to have seen the fabulous Irem, or City of Pillars, and to have found

beneath the ruins of a certain nameless desert town the
shocking annals and secrets of a race older than man-
kind. He was only an indifferent Moslem, worshipping
unknown Entities whom he called Yog-Sothoth and
Cthulhu.

After its composition it was translated into Greek as the
Necronomicon by Theodorus Philetas in AD 950, burnt by
the Patriarch Michael in AD 1050, and translated into Latin
by Olaus in 1228.

Needless to say the whole thing was a jape. There was
no real *Necronomicon*. Lovecraft said in a letter of 1937 that
'the name *Necronomicon* (*necros*, corpse; *nomos*, law; *eikon*,
image = An Image [or Picture] of the Law of the Dead)
occurred to me in the course of a dream, although the etymology is perfectly sound.' Scholars have pointed out that
the etymology is in fact fundamentally unsound, but that
misses the point. It was a game, and a highly entertaining
one. Soon other writers began to join in, quoting from the
nonexistent work and even composing large sections of it
(despite Lovecraft's wise warning that 'if anyone were to
try to write the *Necronomicon*, it would disappoint all those
who have shuddered at cryptic references to it.') Booksell-
ers were plagued by requests for it, and it began to appear
in library card catalogues, doubtless slipped in by librar-
ians who afterwards dissolved into a sticky whitish mass.
Lovecraft himself was often asked if the *Necronomicon* were
real, and always answered patiently in the negative. But
the myth (or mythos) persisted: Lovecraft's friend Robert
Bloch, for example, wrote a short story called 'The Shambler

from the Stars' (1935) in which a young man corresponds with a recluse, 'a mystic dreamer in New England' who tells him of the secret book *The Necronomicon*. The mystic dreamer (obviously Lovecraft) meets a foul end when a spell conjures up a repulsive Thing from another world which seizes him in its tentacles and sucks him dry. Several *Necronomicons* were in fact later published. The best known is probably the so-called 'Simon Necronomicon', which has sold almost a million copies. Not bad for a joke.

In Ecclesiastes we read that 'of the making of many books there is no end:' one might also say that 'of the making of fictional titles there is no end.' Lovecraft had a taste for it,[32] but he is by no means the only one. The attraction of creating a title that stands alone is not hard to see. Inventing a fictional book gives authors all the delight of creating a title without having to go to the bother of writing the actual book. Added to this is the fact that many authors, being naturally self-regarding, write books in which the heroes are themselves authors, which leads naturally on to a listing of their (fictional) works. Into these pseudographs can be thrown everything that is too bizarre, whimsical, absurd or adventurous to try on the reading public – and everything that has been rejected by the author's agent or publisher.

---

32 His other fictional occult books, many bearing improbable clashes of consonants, include the 'Pnakotic manuscripts' and the 'Seven Cryptical Books of Hsan'. Nor was Lovecraft averse to references to real books of great and mysterious antiquity, such as the Egyptian *Book of Thoth*, or merely books of abstruse gibberish, such as Madame Blavatsky's *Book of Dzyan*.

A full list of the fake titles of world literature would be several times as long as this book. One might mention the huge outpouring of fake titles in Rabelais's *Gargantua and Pantagruel* (among them *The Shitabranna of the Maids* and *The Bald Arse or Peeled Breech of the Widows*), and the corresponding outpouring in Laurence Sterne's *Tristram Shandy*. There are fictional titles *passim* in the work of Jorge Luis Borges (*The Book of Sand*, *A First Encyclopaedia of Tlön*) and in that of his disciple Umberto Eco. Robert Bloch went so far as to invent fictional works by a real author in *The Further Adventures of Arthur Gordon Pym* by Edgar Allan Poe. Conan Doyle's Sherlock Holmes was the author of various fictional monographs, among them *On the Study of Tobaccos and their Ashes*. There is *The Theory and Practice of Oligarchical Collectivism* in *Nineteen Eighty-Four* by George Orwell. Vladimir Nabokov invented several books by the fictional author John Shade for his *Pale Fire*. Thomas Pyncheon proved a master of the form with his non-existent *Chums of Chance* series: *The Chums of Chance in Old Mexico*, *The Chums of Chance and the Ice Pirates*, *The Chums of Chance Nearly Crash into the Kremlin*, *The Chums of Chance in the Bowels of the Earth* and *The Chums of Chance and the Caged Women of Yokohama*. Martin Amis got in on the act with his author-protagonist Richard Tull, whose books include *Aforethought* and *Invisible Worms*. In *Misery* by Stephen King, the crippled author Paul Sheldon is hard at work writing *Misery's Return*, an effort that nearly kills him. The incomparable Richard Brautigan, in *The Abortion: An Historical Romance*, invented the authoress Marsha Paterson and her book *Bacon Death*.

The Hitch-Hiker's Guide to the Galaxy by Douglas Adams is both a fictional book and a real book, and Adams's other fictional titles include *How I Scaled the North Face of the Megapurna with a Perfectly Healthy Finger But Everything Else Sprained, Broken or Bitten Off By a Pack of Mad Yaks*. AS Byatt has a developed taste for the genre, with her fictitious titles running into the dozens; Jasper Fforde is another serial offender, his titles including *Wuthering Heights: Masterpiece or Turgid Rubbish?* by Millon de Floss. Many fictional books appear in JK Rowling's Harry Potter series, which of course draws its inspiration from the children's fiction of CS Lewis, whose Mr Tumnus had books on his shelves with titles such as *Is Man a Myth?*, *Men, Monks, and Gamekeepers* and *Nymphs and Their Ways*. Perhaps the greatest of all fictional-titlers (for the present author at least) is Kurt Vonnegut. Many of his fictional books are penned by his alter ego Kilgore Trout, and are usually supplied with helpful plot summaries: they include *The Barring-gaffner of Bagnialto, or This Year's Masterpiece* (which concerns a society in which art treasures are assigned values by spinning a wheel) and *The Money Tree* (in which a species of tree evolves with dollar bills for leaves, which attracts humans to it who kill each other around its roots, providing good fertilizer).

Perhaps this highlights the rather rebellious nature of titles. They are like adolescent children, sometimes a little insecure in themselves, often flamboyantly-dressed, desperately seeking approval. Occasionally they strive to break free from the parent body of work completely and demand consideration on their own merits.

22

Gentlemen Prefer Blondes (1925)
Anita Loos

GENTLEMEN *Prefer Blondes* recounts, in the form of a diary,
four months in the life of Lorelei Lee, good-time girl of Roaring
Twenties New York (though she actually originates from Little
Rock, Arkansas), who makes a trip to Europe with her friend
Dorothy, indulging *en route* her predilection for gentlemen,
champagne and diamonds, with the former as a means to
acquire the latter two. Lorelei, despite being the most bubbly
of airheads, considers herself highly intelligent and refined:

> I mean Mr Eisman is in the wholesale button profession
> in Chicago and he is the gentleman who is known practi-
> cally all over Chicago as Gus Eisman the Button King.
> And he is the gentleman who is interested in educat-
> ing me, so of course he is always coming down to New
> York to see how my brains have improved since the last
> time. [...] So of course when a gentleman is interested in
> educating a girl, he likes to stay and talk about the topics
> of the day until quite late, so I am quite fatigued the next
> day and I do not really get up until it is time to dress for
> dinner at the Colony.

Lorelei cuts a swathe through London (where she finds to her annoyance that 'the boat does not come clear up to London but it stops on the beach and you have to take a train'), Paris (where she demands to know 'the name of the unknown soldier who is buried under quite a large monument'), and Vienna (where she has an interview with 'Dr Froyd', who tells her that all she needs is 'to cultivate a few inhibitions and get some sleep'). A good part of the book's charm lies in the voice of Dorothy, a much sharper operator than Lorelei (despite being a brunette). At one point an officious matron by the name of Lady Beekman demands that Lorelei return a diamond tiara given to Lorelei by her husband, threatening to make a fuss and ruin her reputation if she does not do so:

> So Dorothy spoke up and she said, 'Lady you could no more ruin my girl friend's reputation than you could sink the Jewish fleet.' I mean I was quite proud of Dorothy the way she stood up for my reputation. Because I really think that there is nothing so wonderful as two girls when they stand up for each other and help each other a lot. Because no matter how vigarous [sic] Lady Francis Beekman seems to be, she had to realize that she could not sink a whole fleet full of ships.

The passage that will probably be read in anthologies in a thousand years' time occurs about halfway through Chapter Four:

> I mean a girl has to look out in Paris, or she would have such a good time in Paris that she would not get

> anywheres. So I really think that American gentlemen
> are the best after all, because kissing your hand may
> make you feel very very good but a diamond and safire
> bracelet lasts forever.

In the later musical adaptation (1949) and film (1953) this became, of course:

> A kiss on the hand may be quite continental
> But diamonds are a girl's best friend.

Gentlemen Prefer Blondes was serialized in *Harper's Bazaar* in 1925 and was an enormous success. Edith Wharton acclaimed it as the Great American Novel (one of the few to be written by a woman – see chapter 44), William Faulkner said 'I wish I had thought of Dorothy first,' and Aldous Huxley praised its 'robustly Rabelaisian humour' – though in fact the adjective was a little misplaced, since the sexual content is brilliantly understated, and as Loos herself said, 'there isn't a single line in her story that couldn't be read aloud in a kindergarten.'

The title came about as a result of the author's love for the journalist and satirist HL Mencken (she called him 'Menck'). Anita was jealous when, on a train journey, a blonde by the name of Mae Davis attracted Mencken's attention, as well as that of all the other men on the train:

> In the club car, if she happened to drop the magazine
> she was reading, several men jumped to retrieve it,
> whereas I was allowed to lug heavy suitcases from their
> racks while men, most particularly my husband, failed

to note my efforts. We had to change trains in Chicago
and take the Santa Fe, on which I faced three more days
of being bored by that golden-haired birdbrain. As our
train raced across the plains of the Midwest, I watched
her disorganize the behavior of every male passenger on
board. I tried to puzzle out the reasons why. Obviously
there was some radical difference between that girl and
me, but what was it? We were both in the pristine years
of youth. She was not outstanding as a beauty; we were,
in fact, of about the same degree of comeliness; as to
our mental acumen, there was nothing to discuss: I was
smarter. Then why did that girl so far outdistance me in
allure? Why had she attracted one of the keenest minds
of our era? Mencken liked me very much indeed, but
in the matter of sex he preferred a witless blonde. The
situation was palpably unjust but, as I thought it over,
a light began to break through from my subconscious;
possibly the girl's strength was rooted (like that of
Samson) in her hair. At length I reached for one of the
large yellow pads on which I jot down ideas and started
a character sketch which was the nucleus of a small
volume to be titled *Gentlemen Prefer Blondes*.

Gentlemen Prefer Blondes made Loos rich enough to retire
forever, but such a course was anathema to a girl of her
'mental acumen'. She had already distinguished herself as
one of the most talented screenwriters of the early cinema[33],
and went on to become an acclaimed novelist, memoirist
and adapter of plays for the stage. The 'small volume' was
also followed by a sequel, *But Gentlemen Marry Brunettes*,

33 She had written around 120 screenplays by 1920 and pioneered the art of the subtitle – in
the 1916 movie *His Picture in the Papers*, one character blows up a factory, destroys a police
station, then rests from his labours, as the subtitle reads: 'I will have to resort to violence.'

detailing the further adventures of Lorelei and Dorothy. It did well, though not as well as *Gentlemen Prefer Blondes*. Perhaps the title wasn't quite as good: *Gentlemen Prefer Blondes* is marvellous, with its 3-2-1 syllable structure, the superb irony – given the genesis of it – of the word 'gentlemen' (which works best the first time round), and the fact that pre-marital shenanigans will always outsell the depressing finality of matrimony. Marriage, childrearing and home-life are ultimately a drug on the market, and even though Lorelei gets married at the end of *Gentlemen Prefer Blondes*, somehow we don't believe in it. The strongest relationship in both books is that between Lorelei and Dorothy, and not between either of the two girls and any 'gentleman'. As Lorelei says: 'there is nothing so wonderful as two girls when they stand up for each other and help each other a lot.'

23

To The Lighthouse (1927)
Virginia Woolf

To the *Lighthouse* sold so well in 1927 that it enabled Virginia Woolf to buy a car (a second-hand Singer). Its success still has the capacity to surprise. *To the Lighthouse* is an utterly uncompromising novel, the highest point of high modernism, told from a multitude of viewpoints, in a prose style of great luxuriance, and featuring a plot in which nothing happens except a dinner party and a boat journey. In it, events conventionally considered important – deaths in wars or in childbirth, the collapse of a family's fortunes – are told in parentheses, eclipsed by lyrical descriptions of the curve of a piece of fruit or the beauty of a gold watch.

There is a further layer of obscurity. The whole book is a *roman à clef*. The book's paterfamilias, Mr Ramsay, stands in for Virginia's father, the philosopher Leslie Stephen; and the materfamilias, Mrs Ramsay, is an evocation of Virginia's mother Julia, who died when she was thirteen.[34]

---

34 Her sister Vanessa was amazed at the way the book had caught their mother, writing to Virginia in 1927: 'it seemed to me that in the first part of the book you have given a portrait of mother which is more like her to me than anything I could ever have conceived of as possible. It is almost painful to have her so raised from the dead... It was like meeting her again with oneself grown up and on equal terms and it seems to me the most astonishing feat

Six-year-old James Ramsay is clearly based on Virginia's brother Adrian; Prue Ramsay is drawn from Virginia's half-sister Stella, who died (as Prue does in the book) shortly after her marriage; and Andrew Ramsay from Virginia's brother Thoby. Virginia herself is represented most nearly by Lily Briscoe, a friend of the family who struggles to achieve success as a painter, but Virginia is also present diffusely in some of the others, particularly in the young Cam(illa) Ramsay, who wants to be a writer.

The novel then is an attempt to recapture the author's childhood and family, many of them long dead. It comes as no surprise to learn that the lighthouse too is drawn from Virginia's past. In the novel the Ramsay family take a house on the Isle of Skye in the Hebrides, from which they can see a lighthouse in the bay. This location is based closely on the Stephens' own country retreat, Talland House in St Ives, Cornwall, which looked out onto St Ives Bay and the Godrevy Lighthouse. It was here that Virginia spent all her early summers, where she experienced 'the purest ecstasy I can conceive' walking in the gardens and woods around St Ives and playing cricket (she was known as 'the demon bowler'). And in 1892, aged eleven, Virginia made a trip to the Godrevy Lighthouse, as reported in the nursery newspaper *The Hyde Park Gate News* for Monday 12 September:

---

of creation to have been able to see her in such a way. You have given father too I think as clearly but perhaps, I may be wrong, that isn't quite so difficult... In fact for the last two days I have hardly been able to attend to daily life.'

On Saturday morning Master Hilary Hunt and Master
Basil Smith came up to Talland House and asked Master
Thoby and Miss Virginia Stephen to accompany them to
the lighthouse as Freeman the boatman said there was
a perfect tide and wind for going there. Master Adrian
Stephen was much disappointed at not being allowed to
go.

In the novel James, the stand-in for Master Adrian Stephen,
wishes to visit the lighthouse, but is told by his father that
the expedition will be impossible because the weather will
not be fine ('Had there been an axe handy, a poker, or any
other weapon that would have gashed a hole in his father's
breast and killed him, there and then, James would have
seized it.') James's disappointment in the novel is clearly a
memory of Adrian's disappointment in 1892.

The lighthouse also goes some way towards answering
the question of why the book was so successful in 1927.
The lighthouse bears the weight of a book which otherwise would be in danger of disintegrating into a swarm of
sense-impressions and interior echoes; it gathers round it
the characters' emotions. Mr Ramsay is shown to be right
about the inadvisability of the expedition to the lighthouse
but only at some cost to his relationship with his son and
wife ('Damn you!' he cries at Mrs Ramsay for daring to
question the weather forecast). James, looking at the lighthouse, feels a sense of power despite his father ('he might
do anything, he felt, looking at the Lighthouse and the distant shore'), and when, ten years later, in the third part,
James does go to the lighthouse with his father, it is the

occasion of their partial reconciliation, when his father praises him for landing the boat. Even Lily Briscoe, who stays on shore painting, is allowed her moment of vision because of the lighthouse: the novel concludes as she draws the lighthouse in the centre of her painting.

> With a sudden intensity, as if she saw it clear for a second, she drew a line there, in the centre. It was done; it was finished. Yes, she thought, laying down her brush in extreme fatigue, I have had my vision.

Unsurprisingly for such an important motif, though uncommonly for the author, the title was conceived very early on, before the novel was even started. On the day *Mrs Dalloway* was published, May 14, 1925, Virginia Woolf wrote in her diary that she was 'all on the strain with desire to... get on to *To the Lighthouse*.'

Critics have often focused on the symbolic role of the lighthouse, a tempting angle given the first-edition cover by Vanessa Bell showing a phallic, perhaps even ejaculating lighthouse. Roger Fry assumed the symbolic aspect was important, though confessed he failed to understand it: he said in a letter of 1927 that 'the lighthouse has a symbolic meaning that escapes me.' Virginia replied:

> I meant *nothing* by the Lighthouse. One has to have a central line down the middle of the book to hold the design together. I saw that all sorts of feelings would accrue to this, but I refused to think them out, and

> trusted that people would make it the deposit for their
> own emotions – which they have done, one thinking it
> means one thing another another. I can't manage Sym-
> bolism except in this vague, generalized way.

In repudiating symbolism and emphasizing instead the structural importance of the lighthouse Woolf showed not vagueness but remarkable clarity of vision, considering that Freud was at the height of his reputation – a lesser writer would surely have latched onto a psychoanalytic interpretation. The lighthouse, the real lighthouse, was too central to her aims. At stake was the resurrection of her family and the meaning of her childhood, which was happiness itself. Fashionable games of symbolism were beside the point.

24

Before the Flowers of Friendship Faded Friendship Faded (1931)
Gertrude Stein

THE poetry of Gertrude Stein is not now very well known. Even when it was well known it was not very well known. Stein is now famous for two things: 'A rose is a rose is a rose' and *The Autobiography of Alice B Toklas* (which does not contain a recipe for hashish chocolate brownies). This is a shame, since Stein was one of the most important, influential and stylistically distinctive of all modernist writers. Here is a sample of her prose (or prose-poetry), from *Geography and Plays* (1922):

> They were quite regularly gay there, Helen Furr and
> Georgine Skeene, they were regularly gay there where
> they were gay. They were very regularly gay.
>
> To be regularly gay was to do every day the gay thing
> that they did every day. To be regularly gay was to end
> every day at the same time after they had been regularly
> gay. They were regularly gay. They were gay every day.
> They ended every day in the same way, at the same time,
> and they had been every day regularly gay.

And here a sample of her poetry, this being from 'Stanzas in Meditation' (1922):

> I come back to think everything of one
> One and one
> Or not which they were one
> I won.
> They will be called I win I won
> Nor which they call not which one or one
> I won.
> I will be winning I won
> Nor not which one won for this is one.
> I will not think one and one remember not.

It was not just the Stein manner that left its mark on the literary century. Her Paris salon was a nexus of literary talent, attended by many of the most important modernist writers, notably Ernest Hemingway[35], Ezra Pound and Sherwood Anderson; and, with her brother Leo, she began one of the earliest collections of post-Impressionist and Cubist art, comprising canvases by Gauguin, Von Gogh, Cezanne, Picasso, Matisse and Juan Gris.

In 1927, when Stein was fifty-three years old, she was introduced to a twenty-one-year-old French artist and writer, Georges Hugnet. Hugnet was something of a firebrand, and found great appeal in Stein's work. A close friendship soon

---

35 Hemingway's literary debt to Stein is especially obvious, though Hemingway did a great deal later in life to try and detach himself from her. Wyndham Lewis said: 'One might even go so far as to say that this brilliant Jewish lady had made a *clown* of him by teaching Ernest Hemingway her baby-talk. So it is a pity. And it is very difficult to know where Hemingway proper begins and Stein leaves off as an artist.' Hemingway was reportedly so enraged on reading this (in Sylvia Beach's bookshop) that he smashed a vase to the floor.

developed, with Hugnet translating Stein's *The Making of Americans* into French; Stein, for her part, was flattered by the attention, and deeply desired a French audience for her work (Hugnet's was her first translation into French). The letters they exchanged have the flavour of *billets-doux*, with Stein addressing Hugnet as 'My very dear little George' and saying 'I am deeply touched, really... you use phrases that so perfectly render me that I am most excited... Really, my dear friend, I am very happy to be in your hands...' Stein wrote verses about Hugnet which must be considered love-poetry:

> In the month of May
> What shall I say
> In the month of May
> That I love George
> In my way
> In the month of May
> And in other months.

By 1930, three years after their first meeting, the friendship had progressed to the point where Stein agreed to translate Hugnet's 30-poem sequence *Enfances* into English. It was to be published as a parallel text, at first in an edition of the US literary magazine *Pagany*, and then in book form. At first all went smoothly. Hugnet, after seeing the proposed transla-tions, wrote: 'Wonderful Gertrude, what joy you give me... this is not a translation, this is something else, it is *better*. I more than love this reflection, I dream of it and I admire it. And you return a hundredfold the joy I was able to offer you.' However, when the first proofs of the book appeared, joy evaporated. The two writers could not agree about the prominence each of their names should have on the title page. The publishers planned to present the poems as Hugnet's, with, in smaller letters underneath Hugnet's name, the phrase '*suivi par la traduction de Gertrude Stein*' ('followed by the translation of Gertrude Stein'). Stein, however, insisted that her name should be in the same size type as Hugnet's, since her poems were 'reflections' on Hugnet's work rather than conventional translations; they were works of art in their own right. Hugnet refused to compromise. In her anger Stein cabled the editor of *Pagany*, which had not yet printed the poems, saying that the title *Enfances* should be struck out, and a new title substituted: 'Poems Pritten on Pfances of Georges Hugnet.' The baby-talk of 'Pritten' and 'Pfances' was a deliberate attempt to wreck the seriousness of the venture, and made any agreement on the forthcoming book impossible. In early 1931 Stein pulled out of the book venture completely. In its place she published her Hugnet 'translations' alone, without the original texts. She now gave these guerilla translations a completely new title: *Before the Flowers of Friendship Faded Friendship Faded*, with the subtitle: 'Written on a Poem by Georges Hugnet'. Now she had star billing and it was Hugnet who had been reduced to small type. It was intended to show 'very dear little George' exactly what she thought of him.

For such a neat, cutting and appropriate title – the translations were 'the flowers of friendship' and had been preceded into oblivion by the friendship itself – it is strange that it came ready-made from an experience far removed from the contretemps over the poems. In his memoir *Les Précieux* the historian Bernard Faÿ recalled the title's origin:

> One day, in a restaurant at Bourg-en-Bresse, [Alice Toklas] overheard two French women talking; one said to the other, "Before the friendship faded, the flowers of friendship faded…"[36] Struck by the expression, she translated it for her friend, and Gertrude made it the title of one of her most successful poems.

Other accounts exist from Toklas herself:

> I bought some handmade peach-leaf paper and printed one hundred copies. The title came to Gertrude in the dining room of a hotel at Bourg when two guests of the hotel at two different tables were disagreeing.

But the incident in the restaurant must have occurred some time before the Hugnet debacle, because it was a phrase that Stein had already used in her writing, for example in *A Novel of Thank You* (written in 1925/6 and published posthumously), where the phrase opens Chapter 73:

> Before the flowers of friendship faded friendship faded.
> Sunday makes Monday and Monday Sunday.

It was a title that came ready-made, then, to describe – and enact – the withering of a friendship. Some titles seem to be born for a purpose, to hang in literary non-space until a book can be found for them.

---

36 Strictly speaking, Faÿ's account gives the title a diametrically opposite meaning, but one should not quibble.

25

Interlude 2:
In Praise of Folly by Desiderius Erasmus
A Man's a Man by Bertolt Brecht
Le Peau de Chagrin by Honoré de Balzac
The Golden Ass by Lucius Apuleius
Oh! Calcutta! by Kenneth Tynan
Salt Seller by Marcel Duchamp

THE punning title takes more risks than most. It risks, for example, devaluing the seriousness of the book it attaches to. Or being regarded as a genteel substitute for humour (*A Private Function* by Alan Bennett). Or groaned at. Or met with blank looks. And even if it survives these things, it may become incomprehensible in translation.

Can punning titles overcome these obstacles and become famous and respectable as titles of world literature? I think they can, and as proof, here are six examples.

The first is a learned pun, *In Praise of Folly* (1509) by the humanist scholar Desiderius Erasmus. This book, only seventy pages long, was a best-seller that went into forty-two editions in the author's lifetime, and many more since: it is still his best-known book. Following in the tradition of Latin authors who had composed ironic *Encomia* on such subjects as flies and parasites, it was an extended joke extolling all forms of foolishness, and was written in seven days while Erasmus was staying with his friend Sir Thomas More at More's house at Bucklersbury. In tone, *In Praise of Folly* is rather reminiscent of More's *Utopia*: one is never sure whether the author is being serious or satirical, and there is the strong sense that he does not want you to know. The pun comes in because the original title, *Encomium Moriae*, means both the 'Praise of More' and the 'Praise of Folly' (*moria* = folly). Erasmus explained the genesis of the book in a letter to More: 'What the devil put that into your head? you'll say. Well, the first thing that struck me was your surname More, which is just as near the name of *Moria* or Folly as you are far from the thing itself.' No effort has ever been made to reproduce the pun in the English title, for example by calling it *Mores and Morons*. That would be disrespectful.

For English readers, the title of Brecht's play *A Man's a Man* (1926) has echoes of Rabbie Burns —'A man's a man for a' that'. But, as with *In Praise of Folly*, the original German title has a twist it is impossible to render in English. It is *Mann ist Mann*, which can, in German, be heard either as 'Man Is Man' or 'Man Eats Man', since '*ist*' ('is') and '*isst*' ('eats') are homophones. The play, set in British India, deals with a fish porter who is brainwashed into assuming the identity of a dead soldier, and, as the action progresses, witnesses and commits numerous atrocities. Brecht claimed the play presented a 'new human type... mendacious, optimistic, flexible:' and in the light of current events of 1926 – thousands were joining the Nazis – this was prescient. Man is predatory and cannibalistic, and Germany, under the guise of national renewal, was consuming itself.

Another interesting example of the foreign punning title is Balzac's *Le Peau de Chagrin* (1831), usually translated, inadequately, as *The Wild Ass's Skin*. 'Chagrin' is a pun in French meaning both 'grief' and 'shagreen' (a type of leather made from a wild ass skin); and in the story it is the magic ass's skin, which grants any wish, that ensures that the hero comes to grief.

There is another famous 'ass' title that has a punning element: *The Golden Ass*. This is Lucius Apuleius' 2nd century AD comic novel dealing with the adventures of a man transformed into a donkey. Its original title was simply *Metamorphoses*, but it became known as *The Golden Ass* through the intervention of St Augustine, who assured his readers that this was Apuleius' own name for the book. The ass was 'golden' almost certainly because of a piece of Latin wordplay: *Golden Ass* in Latin is *asinus aureus*, and thus relies for its effect on the close similarity of the words for 'ass' and 'gold'. To get a similar effect in English we would have to call it *The Dinky Donkey* or *The Cool Mule*.

What of the unintentional punning title? Such a category, perhaps surprisingly, does exist. The title of Kenneth Tynan's famously risqué revue *Oh! Calcutta!* (1969) was inspired by a painting by the Surrealist Clovis Trouille (1889-1975). This depicts a reclining woman draped in rich fabrics and revealing a pair of plump buttocks decorated with tattooed fleur-de-lis; it is called *Oh! Calcutta! Calcutta!* (and in fact the title is written on the painting itself, underneath the figure). The choice came about in 1966. Tynan's wife Kathleen was writing an article on Trouille, and knew that Ken admired the *derrière* in question. When she suggested it as the title of his play he accepted with alacrity. What neither Katherine nor Ken knew, however – until later – was that the title *Oh! Calcutta! Calcutta!* was a pun. Calcutta stands in for 'Quel cul t'as!', or 'What an arse you've got!' Similar punning potentialities were of course exploited by Marcel Duchamp in his famous study of a moustachioed Mona Lisa, *L.H.O.O.Q.* ('*Elle a chaud au cul*,' or, 'She's got a hot arse').

And it is to Duchamp that we finally turn. *Salt Seller* (1973; originally published in French in 1958), a collection of Duchamp's writings, is everything the titular enthusiast could desire. It is not an accidental pun; neither is it an inadequately translated pun. It is in fact a pun of a spoonerism. The original title was *Marchand du sel*, which, twisted around in the manner of the Rev. Spooner, is 'Marcel Duchamp', the author of the book. The editors of the English edition, Michel Sanouillet and Elmer Peterson, were clearly men of genius, since they managed to translate the spoonerism by furnishing a pun on 'salt cellar'; and of course 'salt' is a synonym for 'wit' (as in the phrase 'Attic salt'), so that Duchamp is the 'seller of wit' – not a bad description for the founder of conceptual art. *Salt Seller* is full of similar jokes, many in dubious taste, usually penned under the name of Duchamp's female alter ego, the inscrutable Rrose

Sélavy, whose name itself is a tortured pun, meaning both *'Eros, c'est la vie'* ('love, that's life') or *'arroser la vie'* ('make a toast to life').

For Marcel Duchamp, delight in language, and the pun in particular, was one of the chief delights of life.

26

Cold Comfort Farm (1932)
Stella Gibbons

COLD *Comfort Farm* is one of those books that is familiar even if you haven't read it. 'Something nasty in the woodshed' is its most famous catchphrase, but it is present every time anyone makes tongue-in-cheek references to improbable rustic dialect-terms such as 'clettering', 'mollocking', 'sukebind', 'scranleting' and 'mog's-lanthorn' – or mentions parodic yokels with names like 'Urk'. Even the name of the dynastic family of *Cold Comfort Farm*, Starkadder, seems somehow familiar – perhaps because it is echoed in a later comic creation, Rowan Atkinson's Blackadder.

The book recounts the adventures of a young woman, Flora Poste, who has had 'an expensive, athletic and prolonged' education, and wishes to provide for herself by writing a novel. To gather material for this (and to find a temporary roof) she decides to stay with her distant relatives at Cold Comfort Farm, Howling, Sussex. Flora's tentative letter to her aunt Judith elicits the following response:

'DEAR NIECE,

'So you are after your rights at last. Well, I have expected to hear from Robert Poste's child these last twenty years.

'Child, my man once did your father a great wrong. If you will come to us I will do my best to atone, but you must never ask me what for. My lips are sealed.

'We are not like other folk, maybe, but there have always been Starkadders at Cold Comfort, and we will do our best to welcome Robert Poste's child.

'Child, child, if you come to this doomed house, what is to save you? Perhaps you may be able to help us when our hour comes.

'Yr. affec. Aunt,

'J. STARKADDER'

Flora accepts the invitation, and encounters a bucolic zoo of relatives: Judith and Amos Starkadder (he a preacher at the Church of the Quivering Brethren), their sons Reuben and Seth (think Alan Bates in the film of LP Hartley's *The Go-Between*), free-spirited daughter Elfine, ninety-year-old farmhand Adam Lambsbreath, grandmother Ada Doom, who has never recovered from having seen 'something nasty in the woodshed', the four cows Graceless, Aimless, Feckless and Pointless, and the bull Big Business. They are sunk in a brutishness that would have had George Orwell screaming with delight (see chapter 28). Seth tells Flora:

See – we'm violent folk, we Starkadders. Some on us pushes others down wells. Some on us dies in childer-

> birth. There's others as die o'drink or goes mad. There's
> a whole heap on us, too. 'Tes difficult to keep count on
> us. So once a year Grandmother she holds a gatherin',
> called the Counting, and she counts us all, to see how
> many on us 'as died in th' year.

Flora brings her metropolitan ways into their rancid farm life, and attempts to introduce rationality, contraception, psychoanalysis and dress sense into Cold Comfort Farm. In these endeavours she is entirely successful and the novel ends on a note of complete happiness.

Stella Gibbons had a particular satirical target in mind. In the late twenties and early thirties she worked as a journalist for *The Lady* magazine. In her capacity as book reviewer she found herself progressively irritated by the vogue for gloomy novels of rural life, also known as the 'loam and lovechild' genre. These derived in part from Hardy and Lawrence, but had taken on a cheesy life of their own in the productions of Sheila Kaye-Smith (*Green Apple Harvest, Joanna Godden*), Mary Webb (*Precious Bane, The Golden Arrow*), Mary E Mann (*Mrs Day's Daughters, The Patten Experiment*) and others. She began to pen acid reviews of passages such as the following in Edward Charles' *Sand and the Blue Moss*:

> Go out my lad – go out, my lad – turn your face to the
> sun and when it's brown and the girls can love you, love
> them all, and the sun be with you. They'll have children
> every one, and bless you and love you. They'll have
> children and bless you and love you so long as you leave
> 'em alone in the sun – in the sun.

'We are only too willing to leave 'em alone,' she wrote.

One day in January 1931 she was having lunch with her friend Elizabeth Coxhead (later a novelist and biographer), also a journalist at *The Lady*. Stella told Elizabeth that she was writing a take-off of 'all the grim farm novels,' to be called *Curse God Farm*; Elizabeth replied that it was a good idea but that she should change the title and call it *Cold Comfort Farm*. When asked where she had got such a marvellous name, Elizabeth told Stella that it was the name of a place near the Leicestershire village of Stoke Golding, outside Hinckley, belonging to a grammar school where her father was headmaster. Generations of tenants had suffered ruin there and emigrated to Canada. So Stella, recognising that nature always trumps art, and in the hope that the tenants of the real farm would never read the book, changed her title.

The real 'Cold Comfort Farm' still exists. In 2001 the owners, David and Marjorie Abbott, were interviewed by the *Daily Telegraph*. They said they had bought the farm in 1957, and at the time had never heard of Stella Gibbons or her novel. They found the name depressing and changed it to 'Comfort Farm'. But perhaps a spectral presence disapproved. Mrs Abbott said: 'There's a bedroom… but I won't sleep in it. I did once and felt a presence. One of my sons moved in there and felt it, too. Once he said he saw a woman walking through the house when, in fact, it was empty.'

Whether or not there was a curse on Cold Comfort Farm, there was something of a sting in the tale for Stella

Gibbons. Although her first novel sold enough copies to make her comfortable for life – and has never been out of print – she never followed it up with a similar success, despite producing over twenty further novels. Her nephew Reggie Oliver wrote in his 1998 biography of her that she refused to speak the name of the book out loud, and tended to refer to it only elliptically as 'That book', or hum the words 'Hmm Hmm-hmm Hmm'. What can have happened? With the benefit of hindsight it seems obvious: in 1932 Stella Gibbons, with the daring of youth, hit upon a completely unexplored market for parody, a Lawrentian seam just waiting to be mined by a talented enough writer; and this, when married with a perfect title, was enough to create a classic.

Unfortunately, as any parodist will tell you, parody is no basis for a career.

27

Double Indemnity (1936)
James M Cain

DOUBLE Indemnity was first published in 1936 as a serial in the pulp magazine *Liberty*. It tells the story of Walter Huff, insurance salesman, who is persuaded by uber-vamp Phyllis Nirdlinger to help murder her husband to collect on his 'double indemnity' insurance policy. Huff describes the moment when he knows something is wrong:

> I couldn't be mistaken about what she meant, not after
> fifteen years in the insurance business. I mashed out my
> cigarette, so I could get up and go. I was going to get out
> of there, and drop those renewals and everything else
> about her like a red-hot poker. But I didn't do it... what
> I did do was put my arm around her, pull her face up
> against mine, and kiss her on the mouth, hard.

The lovers stage an accident in which the husband appears to fall from the observation car of a moving train. Then Huff finds out that Phyllis has already killed before – several times. Undeterred, he sticks by her and they flee on a boat to Mexico, but, knowing the police will be waiting for them when they dock, they decide to commit suicide by throwing themselves overboard. The book ends as Huff contemplates the sharks that will attend his final moments.

The title came from a real-life murder case. This was the slaying (no other word is possible) of Albert Snyder by his wife Ruth and her lover Judd Gray in 1927.

Ruth Snyder was a thirty-year-old married woman of Queens, New York. In 1925 she began having an affair with a married corset saleman, Henry Judd Gray. The pair decided they would be better off without Ruth's husband, and hatched a plot to kill him. The motive was partly financial. Ruth had taken out a number of high-premium insurance policies on Mr Snyder's life, and one in particular, with the Prudential Life, had a 'double indemnity' clause. This policy, in normal circumstances, would pay out $45,000, but in the event of accident or homicide would yield a much handsomer $90,000. Ruth had tricked Albert into signing some blank forms, and later filled in the details herself. To make sure that her deception went unnoticed, she instructed her postman that all mail from the Prudential was to be delivered to her personally. When any correspondence arrived, Ruth took it and put it in a bank safety deposit box. The postman, George Marks, testified in court to the arrangement, saying that this was Mrs Snyder's right, but adding that none of the other customers on his 585-stop route had ever made a similar request.

The lovers then turned to the task in hand. On Saturday March 19, 1927, after Albert Snyder had retired to bed, Gray, who had been hiding upstairs in the Snyder residence, attacked him as he slept, striking him with a window sash-weight (an iron bar the shape and size of a rolling pin). He then placed a chloroformed pad over his mouth, tied his hands and feet, and, to make sure he was dead, strangled him with a picture wire.[37] The conspirators threw papers and clothes around the house to make it look as if there had been a burglary, and Judd Gray left the scene for Syracuse, in upstate New York, where had arranged an alibi with a friend. But the plot unravelled within hours. Ruth said that the burglar had knocked her unconscious, but there were no bruises to her head. Then, when the name 'Judd Gray' was found in her address book, she panicked and said she had never heard of him. The police, suspecting that Judd Gray was the accomplice, lied and told Ruth that they already had him in custody, and moreover that he had confessed to the murder. Ruth broke down. She confessed her involvement – though only in the planning, not the murder. Gray was then arrested, and also confessed. 'I would never have killed Snyder but for her,' he said. 'She had this power over me. She told me what to do and I just did it.'

Ruth Snyder came in for particularly harsh treatment in the press. The *New York Times* said: 'Four sleepless nights had left little of the attractiveness which she is said to have possessed. Her eyes were red-rimmed. She carried a soiled blue handbag... her half-smiles were a little creepy under the circumstance, but nevertheless they improved her appearance.' The New York *Mirror* said of her: 'She is ice.

---

37 The exact sequence of events was disputed at the trial, one doctor testifying that Mr Snyder had probably been strangled first.

But she is the ice of a filthy garbage-choked stream. If she could be melted down she would be a crawling mass of poisonous things.' The intellectual elite also followed the case. Damon Runyon called it the 'dumb-bell' murder, not because of the murder weapon, but because the perpetrators 'were so dumb!' F Scott Fitzgerald said: '[I]n prison Ruth Snyder had to be hoisted into [the Jazz Age] by the tabloids – she was, as the "Daily News" hinted deliciously to gourmets, about "to cook, *and sizzle*, AND FRY!" in the electric chair.'

In court Ruth and Judd Gray turned on one another. Ruth said that she had not been involved in the murder of Albert, and on the contrary had 'fought to save his life'. Of Gray, she said: 'I was mortally afraid of him. I saw what a terrible man he was.' Gray, on the other hand, although admitting to the murder, made sure Ruth was implicated. 'She took me by the hand and led me down the hall,' he said. 'I struck him on the head, as near as I could see, one blow. Then I hit him another blow. He raised up and started to holler... I was over on top of him. He grabbed me by the tie. I hollered, "Momsie! Momsie! For God's sake help me!" She took the weight and hit him over the head.'

Each of the lovers now had their own defending counsel. Judd Gray's counsel, stressing the sexual undercurrents of the crime, said of Ruth: 'This woman, this particular venomous species of humanity, was abnormal; possessed of an all-consuming, all-absorbing sexual passion, animal lust, which seemingly was never satisfied!' Ruth's counsel said of Judd Gray: 'This miserable filth of the earth is allowed to sit here... and before he makes his squealing appeal for mercy to you... he has defamed that woman!' The jury took only two hours to find Ruth Snyder and Judd Gray both guilty of murder in the first degree. The executions were scheduled for January 12, 1928.

One final circumstance made the case unique. It was strictly forbidden to take photographs in the death cell, but when the day came, a *Daily News* reporter, Thomas Howard, smuggled in a secret camera taped to his ankle. At the moment of Ruth's execution he lifted his trouser leg and pressed a concealed button. The resulting picture showed Ruth Snyder at the moment of her death, and was splashed on the front page of the *Daily News* the next morning. The photo appeared with the headline 'DEAD!' and the caption: 'This is perhaps the most remarkable picture in the history of criminology. It shows the actual scene in the Sing Sing death house as the lethal current surged through Ruth Snyder's body at 11:06 last night. Her helmeted head is stiffened in death, her face masked and an electrode strapped to her bare right leg.'

The Snyder murder case had a massive influence on American popular culture, mainly through the conduit of James M Cain. Both *The Postman Always Rings Twice* (1934) and *Double Indemnity* (1936) were inspired by the Snyder murder case. Both books have elements in common with the case and with each other: there is the adultery, the theme of a *femme fatale*, the financial motive, the lure of planning the perfect crime, the rapid betrayals in custody. Both books were made into blockbuster films[38] in the 1940s, forming the cold heart of the developing *film noir* genre. In *noir* and in the *noir* novel, the police are often challenged not by cases that require complex analysis but by dumb people doing dumb things, acting against their own interests, betraying one another. The 'Double' of *Double Indemnity* signifies not just the insurance payoff but the duplicity of the characters. The protagonists of the new genre were low characters – petty salesmen carrying on cheap affairs in squalid hotels, people down on their luck and isolated, denizens of the paintings of Edward Hopper. In *noir*, in a strange reversal, seediness replaced glamour, and in fact *became* glamour. From the late thirties onwards, seediness is a distinctively American idiom, and Hollywood is a production line for stories of losers, loners, failures and rebels-without-a-cause. The echoes of the Snyder murder case and its *noir* aftermath can still be seen in the botched heists, slummy backdrops and pointless murders of *Reservoir Dogs, The Grifters, Fargo* or *Jackie Brown*.

---

38 In the movie of *Double Indemnity* Walter Huff became Walter Neff, and Phyllis Nirdlinger became Phyllis Dietrichson. The plot was changed to eliminate the flight to Mexico and the suicide pact. Instead, Dietrichson (played by Barbara Stanwyck) tries to kill Walter Neff (played by Fred MacMurray) at the end, and he turns the gun on her. He then dictates his confession to his boss, Barton Keyes (played by Edward G. Robinson).

28

The Road to Wigan Pier (1937)
George Orwell

THE *Road to Wigan Pier* is Orwell's travelogue of the two months he spent in Manchester, Wigan, Sheffield and Barnsley in 1936, investigating housing, going to trades union meetings, descending mines and attending political meetings (he heard Oswald Mosley address a crowd and found him 'a very good speaker'). In Wigan he stayed first with a family he designated in his diary 'the Hs', but after a week moved to lodgings over a tripe shop. 'Social atmosphere very much as at the Hs but house appreciably dirtier and very smelly,' he wrote in his diary. It was exactly what he was looking for. A National Union of Mineworkers official, Jim Hammond, who met Orwell during his stay in Wigan, said:

> He could have gone to any of a thousand respectable
> working-class houses and lodged with them or stayed
> right where he was. But he doesn't do that. He goes to
> a doss-house, just like he's down and out in Paris still.
> You see, when they've left the upper class, they've got to
> go right down into muck and start muckraking... Did he
> have a taste for that sort of thing?

Bernard Crick, writing in 1980, said that this 'doss-house' was still remembered as 'a right filthy hole, a specially filthy hole,' and added that 'Wigan is, to this day, collectively touchy on the tripe-shop issue.' Orwell, however, felt it necessary to experience the greatest degradation on offer, to go 'to labyrinthine slums and dark back kitchens with sickly, aged people creeping round and round them like black beetles,' adding that 'It is a kind of duty to see and smell such places now and again, especially smell them, lest you should forget they exist.'

The experience was a watershed in Orwell's political and literary career. He published altogether nine major works: *Down and Out in Paris and London*, *Burmese Days*, *A Clergyman's Daughter*, *Keep the Aspidistra Flying*, *The Road to Wigan Pier*, *Homage to Catalonia*, *Coming Up for Air*, *Animal Farm* and *Nineteen Eighty-Four*, and the list falls neatly into two halves, pre-*Wigan Pier* and post-*Wigan Pier*. Bernard Crick in his 1980 biography makes the point that it was Orwell's experience of industrial unemployment and poverty that turned him into a committed socialist, and propelled him to fight in Spain that same year; Peter Ackroyd in a *Times* review said that in *Wigan Pier* 'all his anger and frustration found their first proper means of expression.' Orwell himself recognized the shift. In his essay 'Why I Write' (1946) he said: 'The Spanish war and other events in 1936-7 turned the scale and thereafter I knew where I stood. Every line of serious work that I have written since 1936 has been written, directly or indirectly, against totalitarianism and for democratic Socialism, as I understand it.' These 'other events in 1936-7' included the two months he spent in the North.

The Road to Wigan Pier is thus a highly significant book, and from the titular point of view it is one of the more interesting. Orwell's titles tend to be well-made (think of the rhythmic qualities of *Down and Out in Paris and London* or *Keep the Aspidistra Flying*), but on the whole contain little in the way of hidden information. *The Road to Wigan Pier* is an exception.

There is no pier at Wigan, of course: Wigan is inland. The original 'pier' was a gantry carrying coal wagons. This structure, which crossed the main rail line, was made famous before Orwell's time in a music hall joke by George Formby senior (the father of the 'When I'm Cleaning Windows' entertainer). The joke, dating from the early 1890s, has not survived as a quotable entirety, but it ran something like this: some miners are on their way to Southport for a day out, but their train is delayed at the gantry when they wait for the lights to change. One of the miners asks where the bloody hell they are, and receives the reply 'Wigan Pier'. The joke, of course, lies in the contrast between the landlocked industrial wilderness of Wigan and the miners' intended pleasure-grounds on the coast: George Formby is supposed to have added that on his most recent trip to Wigan he had noticed 'the tide was in' – perhaps a reference to the fact that the area, prone to flooding, was under water. The gantry was demolished in the early twentieth century and the location of the famous 'pier' transferred, in the popular imagination, to a small staithe, a ground-level structure, for tipping coal into barges on the Leeds and Liverpool Canal. This in turn was demolished in 1929. Orwell in his book mentions the pier briefly only once, in the form of a regret that he couldn't find it – unsurprising since both the gantry and the staithe had been torn down long before he arrived.

But literary fame can work strange and sometimes appalling transformations. There is now a statue of Winnie-the-Pooh – the Disney version – in White River, Ontario, where a black bear cub later named 'Winnie' was rescued from a hunter and sent to London Zoo. In Wigan, a staithe is still pointed out as representative of the one that Orwell failed to see. It is part of a 'Wigan Pier Experience' project, located in the 'Wigan Pier Quarter', including a pub – named, inevitably, 'The Orwell'. Another pub close by, in the Wetherspoons chain, is named 'The Moon Under Water', in reference to Orwell's famous essay of 1946. There is a Wigan Pier Theatre Company, founded in 1986. A Wigan Pier Nightspot plays house music under the watchful eye of DJ Wiggy. Wigan Pier has also been exported to the sun – there is a Wigan Pier Family Entertainment Bar in Playa De Las Americas, Tenerife.

The tripe-shop never made it to blue-plaque status however. Unlamented, it was demolished in the slum clearances of the 1960s.

29

And Then There Were None (1939)
Agatha Christie

AGATHA Christie had a penchant for nursery-rhyme titles. *One, Two, Buckle My Shoe*; *Three Blind Mice*; *Crooked House*; *Mrs McGinty's Dead*; *A Pocket Full of Rye*; *Hickory Dickory Dock*. The tactic is stark and satisfying: the effect is gained through the contrast between childish innocence and adult iniquity.

And Then There Were None fits the same pattern. It is often cited as the most ingenious of Christie's novels, and Christie herself was especially proud of it. 'It was so difficult to do that the idea fascinated me,' she wrote. 'It was very well received and reviewed, but the person who was really pleased with it was myself, for I knew better than any critic how difficult it had been.' The critics were indeed fulsome: *The Spectator* proclaimed it 'Agatha Christie's masterpiece', and *The Boston Transcript* said: 'For absolute horror and complete bafflement Agatha Christie's *And Then There Were None* takes all prizes.' *The New York Times* said: 'It is the most baffling mystery Agatha Christie has ever written, and if any other writer has ever surpassed it for sheer puzzlement the name escapes our memory.'

The plot concerns ten people from a variety of backgrounds – a general, a judge, a butler, a doctor, a good-looking young man, a good-looking young woman, and other stock properties – who are invited to an island off the coast of Devon. Their common link is that they have all been involved with the deaths of innocent persons, and have either escaped justice or been acquitted of their crime. When they arrive on the island, they find that their hosts, Mr and Mrs Owen, are absent (and in fact they never appear). It is the classic closed-house drama of the kind that Christie liked to work at, and which Tom Stoppard parodied in *The Real Inspector Hound*: no-one can get in or out, and so the murders – and murders there inevitably must be – can only have been committed by a restricted group of suspects.

But it wasn't originally called *And Then there Were None*. What makes this title particularly interesting is that it was originally *Ten Little Niggers*. The island is the consummately un-PC 'Nigger Island' off the coast of Devon. 'He remembered Nigger Island as a boy,' one character muses. 'Smelly sort of rock covered with gulls – stood about a mile from the coast. It had got its name from its resemblance to a man's head – a man with Negroid lips.'

The title came from a Victorian minstrel song published by Frank Green and Mark Mason in 1869, 'Ten Little Niggers'[39], in which ten boys are killed, a subject that seems to have made it popular as a nursery rhyme. In the book, each of the characters finds that a copy of the lyrics has been placed in his or her room. Vera Claythorne, a governess

---

[39] This in turn was based on an American comic song published the previous year, 'Ten Little Indians', by Septimus Winner, which has very similar words.

who has been involved in the death by drowning of one of her charges, encounters it in Chapter Two:

> She stood in front of the fireplace and read it. It was the old nursery rhyme that she remembered from her child-hood days.
>
> Ten little Nigger boys went out to dine;
> One choked his little self and then there were nine.
> Nine little Nigger boys sat up very late;
> One overslept himself and then there were eight.
> Eight little Nigger boys travelling in Devon;
> One said he'd stay there and then there were seven.
> Seven little Nigger boys chopping up sticks;
> One chopped himself in halves and then there were six.
> Six little Nigger boys playing with a hive;
> A bumblebee stung one and then there were five.
> Five little Nigger boys going in for law;
> One got in Chancery and then there were four.
> Four little Nigger boys going out to sea;
> A red herring swallowed one and then there were three.
> Three little Nigger boys walking in the Zoo;
> A big bear hugged one and then there were two.
> Two little Nigger boys sitting in the sun;
> One got frizzled up and then there was one.
> One little Nigger boy left all alone;
> He went and hanged himself and then there were none.

Sure enough each of the murders follows the rhyme: the characters are progressively poisoned, axed, drowned, crushed by a clock in the shape of a bear, etc. – until 'and then there were none.'

But calling the book *Ten Little Niggers* was immediately controversial. Christie's publishers in the USA, Dodd, Mead and Company, refused to issue it as such in 1940 and opted for the last line of the song as a replacement: *And Then There Were None*. 'Nigger Island' became 'Indian Island' throughout. As the twentieth century wore on, the title came to reflect the arc of twentieth-century racial politics. *Ten Little Indians*, hardly much of an improvement, was a common substitute, with the rhyme in the guests' bedrooms in some editions changed to 'Ten Little Soldier Boys'; when adapted as a play and film the work acquired further titles, with one production trying to mend matters by calling itself *Ten Little Redskins*. In 1966, during an English run of the play as *Ten Little Niggers*, civil rights demonstrations were held outside until the producers changed the title to *And Then There Were None*. Even so, *Ten Little Niggers* persisted in Fontana reprints until (quite astonishingly) as late as 1981, and in most foreign-language versions the 'Nigger' element is retained: in Spain the title is still *Diez negritos* and in France *Dix petits nègres*; in Hungarian it is *Tíz kicsi néger* and Romanian *Zece negri mititei*.

It would probably be a mistake to assume that Christie used the word 'nigger' in the title merely as a piece of throwaway racism. She must have seen that her use of the word held an element of unease, even in the 1930s. The little 'nigger boys', after all, are all eliminated in a way that suggests their lives are worth nothing, except as burlesque; precisely, in fact, as slaves or Blacks in the Deep South might be lynched. The title is redolent not so much of the 1930s but of the 1860s – when the song 'Ten Little Niggers' was written – a time when there were ongoing debates about Abolitionism, about the status of the slave, his humanity and worth in comparison to that of his master. In Christie's original title there is casual racism, to be sure, but there is also a deliberate attempt to summon up the ghost of race fear, the spectral presence of the 'other'; none of the substitute titles really matches it. Moreover it is a tension and fear that are intimately and expertly linked to our earliest memories of security, trust and happiness, in the nursery.

30

War with Honour (1940)
AA Milne

ALAN Milne rather resented being known only as the author of *Winnie-the-Pooh*. Most of his writing was for adults. He published numerous successful plays (*Mr Pim Passes By, The Camberley Triangle, The Dover Road, Michael and Mary, The Ivory Door*), novels (*The Red House Mystery, Two People, Four Days' Wonder, Chloe Marr*), verse collections (*Behind the Lines, For the Luncheon Interval, The Norman Church*), essay collections (*Not That It Matters, If I May, Year In, Year Out*), short story collections (*The Secret, Birthday Party, A Table Near the Band*) and books of collected sketches (*The Day's Play, The Holiday Round, Once a Week, The Sunny Side*). But by the time of his death in 1956 Winnie-the-Pooh and his friends had eclipsed them all. In the second half of the twentieth century, helped along by Disney, Pooh would achieve global brand status. It was not what Milne had ever intended or wanted. Most horribly of all, Milne's son, Christopher Robin Milne, hated being the Christopher Robin of the books. He found it difficult, in later life, to forgive his father.

Among the most unexpected of all Milne's adult productions are his writings on international politics, particularly
on the subjects of pacifism and war. Milne had first-hand
experience of war, having served in the 11th Royal War-
wickshire Regiment as a signals officer during World War
One. It was war, the brutal trench warfare of the Somme in
1916, that shaped his political opinions for the rest of his
life. It confirmed his pacifist leanings and led him to write
a book called *Peace with Honour: An Enquiry into the War
Convention*, which appeared in 1934.

Peace with Honour called on Britain to avoid, at all costs,
war with Nazi Germany. The First World War had left a scar
on Europe (and on Milne) which was still far from healing:
in 1934 it was only sixteen years distant. Milne believed
that another world war would bring about the complete
collapse of civilization. He explained:

> I wrote *Peace with Honour: An Enquiry into the War
> Convention* as an ordinary man who hated war. My soul
> revolted against it; my heart revolted against it; but most
> of all my mind revolted against it [...] War, I felt, was not
> the human nature it was so often said to be, but only a
> convention. When two individuals disagree, they go,
> conventionally, to Law. When two nations disagreed,
> and neither would give way, they went, equally conven-
> tionally, to War. I did not see why the convention should
> not be changed, so that they too went to Law.

Milne tried in *Peace with Honour* to undermine notions of
'national honour', and bitterly attacked the way the church

gave its blessing to warmongers on both sides. He pointed out the very much more destructive scale of modern war, and tried, perhaps with an element of having his cake and eating it, to persuade his readers that the dictators of Germany and Italy would never start a war anyway, because they knew they would not survive it. He presented himself as a pragmatist, even above his own strongly-felt pacifism: if it could be proved, he said, that war could be ended *forever* by just one more devastating war, he would have said 'Good, let's start tomorrow. Who do we fight?'

Milne's impassioned and intelligent prose won many converts. *Peace with Honour* achieved sales of 12,000 within the first three months of publication. Its success pleased Milne immensely. He wrote to his American publisher, John Macrae: 'You have always told me that personally you thought more of *Winnie-the-Pooh* than of any book I have ever written. Please let me tell you that I think more of *Peace with Honour* than of any book I have ever written.'

But as the thirties wore on, and the news of fascist evils from Europe became more and more dispiriting, Milne's arguments began to seem less and less adequate. *Peace with Honour* had been written from the viewpoint of a rational man working things out in a sensible way. But it was evident that what was brewing in Europe was a form of lunacy. On the outbreak of hostilities in September 1939, Milne saw that pacifism was now scuppered as a meaningful response to the situation.

His complete break with the arguments of *Peace with Honour* came in 1940 with the pamphlet *War with Honour*.

Its title was intended both as an echo and a refutation of his earlier book. It was published as part of Macmillan's 'War Pamphlets' series which also offered essays such as *Let There Be Liberty* by AP Herbert (Milne's colleague at *Punch*), *Nordic Twilight* by EM Forster, *For Civilization* by CEM Joad and *The Rights of Man* by Harold Laski. 'If anybody reads *Peace with Honour* now,' Milne wrote in *War with Honour*, 'he must read it with that one word "HITLER" scrawled across every page. Before every irresistible conclusion to which I seek to draw him he must insert another premise: HITLER.' The pacifist position that all wars were essentially and depressingly the same, that there were no just wars, and no wars in which one side has more good on their side than the other, was now rejected entirely:

> I believe that Nazi rule is the foulest abomination with which mankind has ever been faced.
>
> I believe that, if it is unresisted, it will spread over, and corrupt, the whole world.
>
> I believe that no decent man, no humane man, no honest man: no man of courage, intelligence or imagination: no man who ever had a kindly thought for his neighbour or compassion for the innocent: no lover of truth, no lover of beauty, no lover of God could have a place in that world.
>
> I believe, therefore, that it is as much the duty of mankind to reject such a world as it is the duty of any community to reject gangster rule.
>
> I see no way of doing this save by the use of force.
>
> I am not frightened by words. If this use of force be called International War, then for the first time in my life

> I approve of International War; if it be called Civil War, then, not for the first time, I approve of Civil War. If it be compared with the action of policemen, then, as often before, I am in favour of action by policemen. If it be called Resistance to Evil, then, as (I hope) always, I am for resistance to evil.
>
> Only when we have resisted it and overcome it can Civilization resume its march.

By the early 1940s Milne's writing had become almost entirely war-orientated. He became a prominent foe of his erstwhile colleagues in the peace movement. He attacked those such as PG Wodehouse who he thought were not warlike enough (see chapter 36). He supported wartime censorship at the BBC. He attacked the anti-Churchill People's Convention. He joined the Home Guard, and even pulled strings to send his son Christopher Robin off to fight, as far as he knew to the same trenches he had endured in 1916. (Christopher Robin served in North Africa and Italy in the Royal Engineers, and survived the conflict.)

The journey from *Peace with Honour* in 1934 to *War with Honour* in 1940 took all of Milne's intellectual and moral resources. In the peace movement, Milne had been lauded and looked up to (and had sold books – what greater temptation?). The easiest course, perhaps, would have been to have kept toeing the pacifist line. Instead, he admitted publicly that he had been wrong, and suffered the inevitable accusations of hypocrisy and backsliding.

But this journey and transformation, perhaps the most important of his life, now registers barely a ripple. AA

Milne is known for one thing and one thing only. We all know who won World War Two, after all: whether AA Milne was on the side of the appeasers, the conscientious objectors or the war party is not now of much interest. The true all-conquering armies, that rolled over everything AA Milne wrote, thought or did, were the denizens of the Hundred Acre Wood.

31

You Can't Go Home Again (1940)
Thomas Wolfe

THOMAS Wolfe (1900-1938) was one of the giants of early twentieth-century letters. Literally so, since he was six feet six inches tall, heavily built, could change a light-bulb from a standing position, and was in the habit of using the top of his refrigerator as a desk. His first, and best-known book, was *Look Homeward, Angel* (1929), a book that influenced the course of the American novel: traces of it can be glimpsed in writers such as Kerouac, Bellow and Roth. He named it after a line in Milton's *Lycidas*:

> Look homeward, Angel now, and melt with ruth:
> And, O ye Dolphins, waft the hapless youth.

The choice of a quotation featuring the words 'home' and 'angel' was appropriate, since the novel was essentially a *bildungsroman* detailing, with great exactness, Wolfe's early years in the small town of Asheville, North Carolina, where his father, a funerary stonemason, kept a seven-foot angel in Carrara marble on the porch outside his shop. Life in a small town à la Sinclair Lewis's *Main Street* offered Wolfe tempting targets for satire. His goal was to write something 'in places terrible, brutal, Rabelaisian, bawdy.' He intended to expose Asheville – renamed Altamont in the book – its snobberies, hypocrisies, the hysterical greed brought about by the real-estate boom of the 1920s, where the whorehouse was an institution at the centre of civic life, where all was 'pain, ugliness, misunderstanding and terror'. His own family came in for particular attention. In the novel the Wolfes became the Gants: Thomas Wolfe himself was the hero Eugene Gant, and the book's paterfamilias, WO Gant, was based on Wolfe's own father. Wolfe wrote in a letter:

> The sad family of this world is damned all together,
> and joined, from its birth in an unspoken and grievous
> kinship: in the incestuous love of sons and mothers; in
> Lesbic hungers and parricidal hatreds; in the terrible
> shames of sons and fathers, and the uneasy shifting of
> their eyes; in the insatiable sexuality of infancy, in our
> wild hunger for ourself, the dear love of our excrement,
> the great obsession of Narcissus, and in the strange first
> love of every boy, which is for a man.

So his declaration at the beginning of the book, 'To the Reader', is patently ridiculous:

> This note [...] is addressed principally to those persons
> whom the writer may have known in the period covered
> by these pages. [...] Now that it is to be published, he
> would insist that this book is a fiction, and that he medi-
> tated no man's portrait here.

A more mendacious foreword is difficult to imagine – unless it be Hemingway's foreword to *The Sun Also Rises*.[40]

Wolfe knew that *Look Homeward, Angel* would cause problems, and began responding to criticism before the novel was even published, drafting letters to the editors of the Asheville newspapers rebutting potential claims that he had done anything to cause offence. And indeed when the criticisms came they were much as he had anticipated. The book caused uproar. The Asheville press attacked it as being full of 'lurid details of blood and sex and cruelty' and claimed it was written as an act of contempt: 'North Carolina, and the South, are spat upon.' Wolfe received poison-pen letters and death threats. One respectable lady said she would not intervene if a lynch-mob dragged his 'big overgroan karkus' through the streets. One overheard comment reported to Wolfe was: 'I talked to so-and-so and he doesn't give a damn how big the whipper-snapper is – if he comes back to this town they'll tear him to pieces.' Another resident – who may have been portrayed in the novel – begged to the librarian: 'Do not let this bucket of night-soil sit upon your shelves.'

Meanwhile, in the wider world, *Look Homeward, Angel* received very favourable reviews, and Wolfe, living in the safety of New York, became a literary celebrity. He told a friend that he was pursued day and night by women crying 'Fuck me, fuck me.' He drew up a list headed 'Free Pieces of Cunt', and said 'I fucked these women for nothing – save the best price of all.'

---

40 See *Why Not Catch-21?* (Frances Lincoln, 2007)

It ultimately failed to solve his problems. He did not go home for eight years. When he did finally pluck up the courage to visit, in 1937 – he made two attempts, going south in stages, feinting towards Asheville and withdrawing – the fuss had died down. The Depression had taken its toll, and many of the people he had pilloried had died or moved away. Wolfe found, to his great relief, that he was forgiven. He was even invited to address the Asheville Business Club, and told them: 'If anything I have written has displeased anyone in my home town, I am genuinely and sincerely sorry for it.' Nevertheless he realized that his connection to his birthplace had been severed forever. Too much time had passed, and too many changes had taken place. Only the mountains, he observed, had remained the same.

During the eight years he had been away, Wolfe had been working on his second novel. He wrote prolifically, incontinently, almost, to the increasing despair of his editor, Maxwell Perkins (also the editor of Hemingway and Fitzgerald).[41] Wolfe's ambition for his second novel was to produce 'one of the longest books ever written', along the lines of *A la recherche du temps perdu* or *War and Peace*, and when he finally submitted the manuscript to Perkins – in fact Perkins had to wrestle it off him, because Wolfe was adding to it at the rate of thousands of words a day – it was about a million words long, forming a pile of paper two feet high. Maxwell mined it for a much-reduced book of 912 pages called *Of Time and the River*, dealing with the

---

41 Perkins arranged meetings between Wolfe and Hemingway and Wolfe and Fitzgerald, partly in an attempt to get them to persuade Wolfe to edit more carefully. Hemingway was appalled by Wolfe's huge size and prolixity, and described him as 'a glandular giant with the brains and the guts of three mice... the over-bloated Lil Abner of literature.'

later adventures of Eugene Gant, which was published in 1935. But there was much more material in the paper-mine, and later editors carved two further novels out of it: these were *The Web and the Rock* (1939) and *You Can't Go Home Again* (1940), both published posthumously[42].

You Can't Go Home Again was in some ways a discrete entity despite the fact that it was submerged in the mass of paper. The plot followed the fortunes of George Webber, a tyro novelist, who produces a book that satirizes the inhabitants of his home town, Libya Hill, and consequently receives death threats and poison pen letters. He does go home and is bitterly attacked. Later sections deal with Webber's further adventures in New York, Paris and Berlin, and Webber finally returns to the USA with the consciousness that his previous actions and the passage of time have made it impossible for him to truly 'go back'.

Wolfe himself chose the title, despite the fact that he was dead when the book was extracted and published. At a dinner with the Communist activist Ella Winter, in 1937, he told her of 'his horror at going back to his home and what he found there,' and she commented, 'But don't you know you can't go home again?' Wolfe asked her: 'Can I have that? I mean for a title... I'm writing a piece... and I'd like to call it that. It says exactly what I mean.' And in the last drafts of the book this passage appeared:

> You can't go back home to your family, back home to
> your childhood, back home to romantic love, back home

---

42 Another book, *The Hills Beyond* (1941), which contained various short fictions, also came from the paper-mine.

to a young man's dreams of glory and of fame, [...] back
home to the ivory tower, back home to places in the
country, to the cottage in Bermuda, away from all the
strife and conflict of the world, back home to the father
you have lost and have been looking for, back home to
someone who can help you, save you, ease the burden
for you, back home to the old forms and systems of
things which once seemed everlasting but which are
changing all the time – back home to the escapes of Time
and Memory.

Winter's phrase, he felt, expressed 'a pretty tremendous
fact and revelation'.

Rather neat: Wolfe's first book had, by its very existence,
created the conditions necessary for his final one to be
written.

32

She Came to Stay (1943)
Simone de Beauvoir

AUTOBIOGRAPHY is often the first blush of fiction. In their early careers writers tend to hitch a ride on real life, and only later find the strength to actually make things up. Think of Wolfe's *Look Homeward, Angel* (see the previous chapter), Hemingway's *The Sun Also Rises* (which pillories his friends of the 1920s), or Huxley's *Crome Yellow* (which satirizes the Garsington set of Ottoline Morrell). These first novels are so autobiographical as to be outright *roman à clef*s. And the same is true of the first novel of Simone de Beauvoir.

She Came to Stay was published before *The Second Sex* (1953), *The Mandarins* (1954), *Memoirs of a Dutiful Daughter* (1959) or any of de Beauvoir's other works of fiction, theatre, philosophy or criticism, at a time when her career so far had involved teaching at a girls' school in Rouen. The novel, whose French title is *L'Invitée*, deals with a couple, Françoise Miguel (a writer), and Pierre Labrosse (an actor), whose relationship is disrupted by the arrival of a beautiful, footloose younger woman, Xavière. Françoise and Pierre are both strongly drawn to Xavière, and they 'invite' her into the relationship, attempting a *ménage à trois*. But the young woman begins playing the older couple off against one another. Françoise's jealousy starts to spiral out of control:

> She was struck with a wild desire to thrash Xavière, to trample upon her. She spent hours listening patiently to her duets with Pierre, and Xavière was refusing her the right to exchange the slightest token of friendship with him! That was too much. It could not go on in this way. She would stand it no longer.

Françoise ends up gassing her rival:

> She stood staring at Xavière's door: alone; unaided; relying now entirely on herself. She waited for some time. Then she walked into the kitchen and put her hand on the lever of the gas meter. Her hand tightened – it seemed impossible. Face to face with her aloneness, beyond space, beyond time, stood this alien presence that had for so long overwhelmed her by its blind shadow: Xavière [...] She repeated 'She or I.' She pulled down the lever.

Almost everything in the novel was based on life. Françoise was de Beauvoir; Labrosse was Jean-Paul Sartre, de Beauvoir's lover; and Xavière was one of de Beauvoir's students at the girls' school, Olga Kosakiewicz. Only the gas was a fiction.

Olga was of Russian ancestry, and was nicknamed by the teachers *La petite Russe*. De Beauvoir said that from her first meeting with Olga she 'savoured the special charm of her features and gestures, her voice, her speech, and special way of talking... There was an impetuous, whole-hogging streak in her that I found most disarming.' De Beauvoir was twenty-seven, and Olga seventeen. Sartre, who was thirty, met Olga in 1935 through de Beauvoir, and soon also fell under her spell. They embraced her as part of 'the Family', a coterie – with cultic resonances – of students they had collected around them. Several members of the Family moved into a hotel in Rouen together, where the corridors at night continually 'echoed to amorous sighing'.

In fact the idea of adopting a young girl and absorbing her into their relationship had long been a fantasy of Sartre and de Beauvoir's. Such an act might be, they theorized, a route to self-examination, an opportunity to plumb the depths of their own sexual/emotional strengths and weaknesses. 'We thought that human relationships remained perpetually to be made up as you go along,' de Beauvoir later wrote. And yet, once it became a reality, de Beauvoir could not help feeling that, whatever joy and self-knowledge it might bring, the trio existed chiefly for Sartre's pleasure. 'The edifice as such was Sartre's work,' she wrote. 'For my own part, though I vainly tried to achieve satisfaction from the relationship, I never felt at ease with it.' Sartre had informed de Beauvoir at the outset of their relationship that he did not intend to restrict himself to any one woman, and de Beauvoir was determined to reciprocate, to show that she too could play the male game. 'The individual who is a subject, who is himself... endeavours to extend his grasp on the world... For woman, to love is to relinquish everything for the benefit of a master,' she wrote later in *The Second Sex*. The absorption of Olga was an attempt to repudiate the 'master' and gain 'mastery'. In short, Simone thought that she could handle it. 'I knew to what extent Sartre was obstinate about the project that governed his entire existence: to know the world and to express it. I was so certain of being intimately linked to this central concern of his, that no episode in his life could frustrate me.' But she had not bargained on Sartre's own catastrophic loss of control. 'Sartre let himself go,' de Beauvoir wrote, 'to the great detriment of his emotional stability, and experienced feelings of alarm, frenzy and ecstasy such as he had never known with me.' Sartre wrote: 'Each day I used to wait for the moment of seeing her again – and beyond that moment for some kind of impossible reconciliation. The future of all these moments... was this impossible love.' Olga, as Xavière does in the novel, was not just disrupting the relationship between Simone and Jean-Paul but threatening to destroy it. 'Whenever I thought of the trio as a long-term project, stretching ahead for years,' de Beauvoir wrote, 'I was frankly terrified.' And Olga was fickle, transferring her affections from one to the other, hoping to excite jealousy and gain control. One day she ground a lit cigarette into her hand, 'pressing it into the flesh with a positively maniacal concentration' – perhaps an attempt to express the nihilism they had descended into.

De Beauvoir moved to Paris, and Olga followed. Sartre was by now finding release from his feelings by pursuing other young women, but de Beauvoir was still traumatized. She began meditating a novelized treatment of the situation as an attempt at therapy. The idea was suggested by Sartre himself. De Beauvoir wrote in her autobiography:

> 'Look,' he said, with sudden vehemence, 'why don't you put yourself into your writing?'... I felt as though someone had banged me hard on the head. 'I'd never dare do that,' I said. To put my raw, undigested self into a book, to lose perspective, compromise myself – no, I couldn't do it. I found the whole idea terrifying. 'Screw up your courage,' Sartre told me, and kept pressing the point. I had my own individual emotions and reactions; it was these that I ought to express in my writings. As happened whenever he put himself behind a plan, his words conjured up a host of possibilities and hopes; but I was still afraid. What in fact was I afraid of? It seemed to me that from the moment I began to nourish literature with the stuff of personality, it would become something as serious as happiness or death.

The novel was originally entitled *Self-Defence*, which makes it clear quite how important it was to the survival of de Beauvoir's sense of her own identity. 'If I was to overcome,' she wrote, 'on my own account that solitary wilderness into which I had flung Françoise, I must work my fantasy through to the bitter end.' The bitter end included a murder. One might have thought that this fictional murder could not be discussed with Olga as it was being written, but such was the enmeshing of their lives at this point that

She Came to Stay was actually dictated to Olga as amanuensis – and dedicated to her.

The Olga-de Beauvoir-Sartre triangle was finally defused by war (Sartre was drafted), by Sartre's ability to find new women (one of whom was Olga's younger sister Wanda) and by Simone's catharsis in the writing of *She Came to Stay*. The novel was published in 1943 and was an immediate success, selling out its 23,000 wartime print-run. It was a moment of enormous importance to de Beauvoir, enabling her to emerge as a writer from under the shadow of Sartre, and laying the groundwork for her career. As for Olga, she continued to be a friend of both Sartre and de Beauvoir, and in 1941 married Jacques-Laurent Bost, one of the other key members of the Family – who also happened to be de Beauvoir's lover. It was yet another example of the philosophy that human relationships were a matter of perpetual experimentation.

33

The Glass Menagerie (1944)
The Rose Tattoo (1950)
Tennessee Williams

TENNESSEE Williams' sister Rose suffered from life-long mental illness, and underwent a pre-frontal lobotomy in 1937. The operation was new and untested, and in Rose's case was a disastrous failure, leaving her permanently brain-damaged. She spent the rest of her life in institutions, unsure who she or her family were, and convinced that she was forever twenty-eight years old. Tennessee Williams' attempt to explore the tragedy of Rose gave rise to many of his greatest plays, and Rose herself appears in various guises throughout his work.

The Rose-theme begins with Tennessee Williams' earliest major work, *The Glass Menagerie*. This play has its origins around 1941 as a short story called 'Portrait of a Girl in Glass'; it was later expanded into a screenplay entitled *The Gentleman Caller*, before becoming *The Glass Menagerie* in 1944. The play follows the fortunes of the Wingfield family, who live a drab existence in a cramped flat in St Louis, Missouri. Amanda, the matriarch, aspires to a life of delicate Southern gentility, but this has long ago become impossible; her husband has long since deserted her and left her to bring up her two children, now in their twenties. These are Tom, a warehouseman with literary aspirations, and Laura, a mentally-fragile young woman with a limp who seeks solace in her collection of little glass animals. Laura's nickname in the play is 'Blue Roses', a reference to a bout of pleurisy (pleuroses/blue roses) she'd had as a youngster. When one day Tom brings his friend Jim home from work, Amanda makes lavish preparations, hoping Jim might make a husband for Laura, and things appear to augur well when Laura realizes that Jim is the young man she'd fallen in love with at school. Amanda and Tom leave Laura and Jim together for a sultry evening, but Jim reveals that he is engaged to be married. Before leaving he accidentally knocks over and breaks one of Laura's glass animals (a unicorn). After he has gone Amanda rounds hysterically on Tom, accusing him of bringing Jim home under false pretences, saying that Tom must have known all along about the engagement. The play ends as Tom addresses the audience, from the perspective of several years in the future:

> Oh, Laura, Laura, I tried to leave you behind me, but
> I am more faithful than I intended to be! I reach for a
> cigarette, I cross the street, I run into the movies or a bar,
> I buy a drink, I speak to the nearest stranger – anything
> that can blow your candles out! For nowadays the world
> is lit by lightning! Blow out your candles, Laura – and so
> good-bye.

'Tom' was Tennessee himself ('Thomas' was Tennessee's original name); 'Amanda' was his mother, also a heroically-declining Southern Belle; and 'Laura' was his sister Rose, who did indeed own a menagerie of little glass animals. Tennessee said in an interview with the *New York Times* in 1945 that the play was:

> semi-autobiographical, based on the conditions of my life in St Louis. The apartment where we lived wasn't as dingy and poverty-stricken as that in the play, but I can't say much for it, even so. It was a rented, furnished apartment, all over-stuffed furniture, and the only nice room in it was my sister's room. That room was painted white and she had put up a lot of shelves and filled them with little glass animals. When I'd come home from the shoe place where I worked – my father owned it, I hated it – I would go and sit in her room. She was the member of the family with whom I was most in sympathy, and, looking back, her glass menagerie had a meaning for me. Nostalgia helped – it makes the little flat in the play more attractive really than our apartment was – and as I thought about it the glass animals came to represent the fragile, delicate ties that must be broken, that you inevitably break, when you try to fulfill yourself.

Tennessee's brother Dakin went further and said it was 'a virtually literal rendering of our family life at 6254 Enright Avenue, St Louis, even though the physical setting is that of an earlier apartment, at Westminster Place. There was a real Jim O'Connor, who was brought home for my sister. The Tom of the play is my brother Tom, and Amanda Wingfield is clearly my mother.'

The glass animals represent the fragility of his sister Rose, her sad attempt at feminine delicacy in a rundown flat, and the bonds that must be broken if anyone is to find personal freedom.

Tennessee never forgave his parents for authorizing the lobotomy that left Rose so scarred, and continued writing about Rose for the rest of his life. The desire to document the tragedy of Rose can be seen clearly in *The Glass Menagerie*, but it is also present in plays such as *The Purification, The Two-Character-Play* and *Suddenly Last Summer*, in which one character, Catherine, is also threatened with a lobotomy. In his play of 1950, *The Rose Tattoo*, roses break out everywhere, almost like plague-sores.

The Rose Tattoo[43] deals with the delle Rose family, immigrants of Sicilian origin: mother Serafina, daughter Rosa, and dead husband Rosario, who in life had borne a rose tattoo on his chest. Serafina has spent the years after her husband's death worshipping his memory, even setting up a shrine to him in the corner of the living-room (which has rose-patterned wallpaper). At the same time she attempts to control her daughter Rosa, who is developing into a young woman of healthy romantic and sexual appetite. Half-way through the play Serafina discovers that her beatified husband was in fact a serial adulterer, and in her anger and humiliation sets the rest of the play's events in motion.

---

43 Other titles considered included *Novena to a Rose, A Candle to a Rose, A Rose for Our Lady, The Grace of Our Lady, A Rose from the Hand of Our Lady* and *Perpetual Novena to a Rose.*

The ghost of Tennessee's sister Rose is present through-out, and not just in the ubiquitous floral imagery. The central situation, of a repressive mother striving to rein in a sexually-developing young daughter, has a clear paral-lel in the relationship between Tennessee's mother and his sister. Tennessee said more than once that Rose's problems were fundamentally ones of sexual repression. Rose, in wild outbursts, would often rave about sex, and Tennes-see was convinced that this was (at least partly) the reason why his mother gave the permission for the lobotomy. 'I think she was frightened most of all by Rose's sexual fan-tasies,' Tennessee said. 'My sister was such a vital person. She could have become quite well by now if they hadn't performed that goddam operation on her; she would have come up back to the surface. My mother panicked because she said my sister had begun using four-letter words. "Do anything! Don't let her talk like that!"'

Tennessee Williams' plays can therefore be seen as a sort of shrine to Rose, and indeed he did set up a literal shrine to his sister later in life, an actual altar in his home created as a deliberate echo of the altar Serafina sets up to her dead husband Rosario: on it he placed Rose's picture as well as a portrait if St Jude, the patron saint of lost causes. Perhaps part of the reason was that he knew himself to be mentally fragile. He had suffered a mental breakdown and hospital-ization in 1935, and was a lifelong sufferer from depression and suicidal thoughts. Add to that the guilt and shame of his failure to do anything for Rose in 1937, and there are all the materials for a potent sister-cult.

34

Whisky Galore (1947)
Compton Mackenzie

WHISKY *Galore* tells the story of what happens when a ship called the 'SS Cabinet Minister', carrying a cargo of 50,000 cases of whisky, founders between the islands of Great and Little Todday in the Hebrides in 1941. The liquor-starved islanders get a jump on the customs officials and appropriate the whisky; later they are pursued by the authorities in the form of Home Guard Captain Paul Waggett. The novel was a best-seller and was made into a film of 1947, also by the title of *Whisky Galore!* (with an exclamation mark).

As is well known, the story is based on fact, though the truth is slightly stranger. In February 1941, during the height of the Battle of the Atlantic, a real ship, the 8,000-ton *SS Politician*, was en route to New Orleans and the West Indies from Liverpool. She was loaded with trade goods of all descriptions: machetes, baths, flycatchers, carpets, tobacco, biscuits, telephones, exercise books, medicines, soap, confectionery and banknotes. These latter, in the form of eight cases of Jamaican ten shilling, one pound and five pound notes, worth around 100 million pounds in today's money, were being sent under conditions of great secrecy from a British printers to Kingston, Jamaica. But there was something aboard the *Politician* worth more even than banknotes: whisky. Around 22,000 cases of it. Bombing raids on Scottish distillery warehouses had forced the owners to move the fluid to safer ground, and a decision had been taken to export it to the American luxury market.

On February 3 the *Politician* left port and steamed northwards to the Hebrides, hugging the coast so as to avoid German U-boats. The plan was to turn left at Scotland and skip across the Atlantic. But on the night of February 5, bad weather blew up between the Hebridean islands of Barra and Eriskay. The Politician struck a reef and ruptured her oil tanks. The following morning the situation was desperate, and the crew abandoned ship and made for Barra. The *Politician* was left on the reef, immovable, though intact. An official salvage operation was quickly mounted, and by February 11 everything considered of value had been taken off by the authorities. Large quantities of goods, however, were left on board. Sea water and oil had flooded the hold and the wooden crates had expanded, jamming them together and making them difficult to prize apart. No guard was mounted on what remained.

On the departure of the salvage vessel, a flotilla of boats appeared in the Sound of Eriskay. The islanders – from Mull, Skye, Lewis, Harris, Barra and Eriskay – had more patience with the complex task of salvage. Entering the hold, they broke up the crates and shipped out anything they could carry. Technically their actions were illegal, particularly as regards the whisky, since no duty had been paid on it (it was for the export market), and thus anyone consuming it would be stealing revenues from the state. Some bottles were hidden in lobster-creels and sunk in the bay; others were put into rabbit-holes; yet more were buried under growing crops. But there was so much whisky that hiding-places began to run out. One islander, John MacPherson, a friend of Compton Mackenzie, told the story of a friend of his:

> Now in the twilight this certain night Ronald filled a sugar bag which would contain three or four cases, and he put the whole show on his back, and he made an attempt to move his stock out of the house and hide it in the hill. Ronald was very tired of the bag before he reached his destination, and when he made himself believe that he was in the safest spot in Eriskay for hiding the lot, he let go the bag and emptied it all out.
>
> Now next he got hold of a bottle and he tried to hide it into the corner of a rabbit burrow – and lo and behold, what happened. It struck against another one! Well, he tried it not far from the same place, and the same thing happened, and for six occasions in succession: Ronald could not get his bottle into a burrow because there was one there before him.

There was so much whisky that old ladies bathed their feet in it to cure their rheumatism. Indeed the whisky of the *Politician* was believed to have almost magical properties. You could drink it all day and all night without getting a headache.

As for the remaining non-alcoholic cargo of the Politician, that too was put to good use. Bathtubs were installed in the crofts, despite there being no running water. Many homes received new linen curtains. The Jamaican banknotes were largely ignored, except for use as paper towels to clean oil from the hands of the men attempting to get to the whisky.

Unfortunately the Customs and Excise decided to take a hard line on the 'looters', and several islanders found in possession of whisky, especially if they had oil-covered clothing, were given short jail terms. As many as 2,000 cases, or 24,000 bottles of whisky, worth many thousands in lost duty, had gone missing. Much more whisky – perhaps several thousand cases – remained on the *Politician*, and the authorities decided to dynamite the ship to prevent any further pilfering. This almost unforgivable act was carried out on August 6, using sixteen sticks of gelignite.

This is the story of *Whisky Galore*, but one other titular story is worth telling. When the book was made into a film in 1947, it was felt that the title was not quite right for the American market. In fact the title was composed of two words originating in Scottish Gaelic: *uisge beatha* meaning whisky (literally 'water of life') and *gu leòr* meaning 'in abundance'. (The word 'galore' was not at all well known until the publication of the book, and its previous citation in the *Oxford English Dictionary* comes from as far back as 1863.) Given the obscurity of the title, the eventual substitute in the USA was *Tight Little Island*. Some time after the film was released, however, the humourist James Thurber met the producer of the film, Monja Danischewsky, and said that he regretted he had not been consulted before the title change. The only possible title for the American market, Thurber said, was 'Scotch on the Rocks'.

35

Hurrah for St Trinian's (1948)
Ronald Searle

GANGS of pre-pubescent females wearing stockings and suspender belts and brandishing hockey sticks, engaged in playing pool, getting drunk, smoking, betting, bathing naked in fountains and summoning the devil, as well as stabbing, hanging, shooting, drowning, injecting, torturing, strangling, crushing and impaling each other: such are we likely to find at St Trinian's, the school created by the cartoonist Ronald Searle in a series of drawings from the early 1940s.

The idea began rather innocently in 1941. Searle, just out of art college, was drafted into the Royal Engineers, and stationed at Kirkcudbright, where he made friends with a family called the Johnstons. The two Johnston daughters, Cécilé and Pat, attended a school for girls in Dalkeith Rd, Edinburgh, called St Trinnean's Academy for Young Ladies. The building was a Gothic pile run by a headmistress called Catherine Fraser Lee, who followed the Dalton system of self-led learning, later parodied in the films: 'In other schools girls are sent out quite unprepared into a merciless world, but when our girls leave here, it is the merciless world which has to be prepared.'

To amuse Cécilé and Pat, Searle drew a cartoon in which several girls are clustered around a noticeboard, on which a notice reads: 'Owing to the international situation, the match with St Trinian's has been postponed.' Cécilé and Pat liked the cartoon, and Searle decided to submit it to the magazine *Lilliput* (then under the editorship of Kaye Webb). But before Searle could receive a reply, he was posted abroad, and arrived in Malaya two months later. He took part in the disastrous retreat from Japanese land forces that ended with the surrender of Singapore. But shortly before being captured, Searle found an abandoned copy of *Lilliput* in the street, and saw his cartoon in it.

While in Changi prison camp in Singapore, and as a slave-labourer on the Thai-Burma Railway, Searle made a series of sketches later collected into a celebrated prison diary, showing all the cruelty of the conditions under the Japanese. He also drew more St Trinian's cartoons. All of this work had to be done in secret, and the finished drawings hidden under the mattresses of men with cholera so that the Japanese guards would not discover them. Whereas the first St Trinian's cartoon had been an amusing comment on the microcosmic nature of life in a girls' boarding school, the second and third cartoons were informed by the brutality of POW life, and concerned themselves respectively with arson and lynching ('Well that's O.K. – now for old "Stinks"'). They were published in 1946, when Searle returned from Changi with his cartoons and drawings miraculously intact, and submitted them once more to Kaye Webb – who also later became his wife.

Hurrah for St Trinian's was the first St Trinian's book. It was an immense success, and was followed by further collections such as *The Female Approach* (1949) and *Back to the Slaughterhouse* (1951). Hattie Jacques appeared in *It's That Man Again* as the Trinianesque Sophie Tuckshop, and St Trinian's revues were perfomed at Oxford. St Trinian's girls appeared on radio, in cookbooks, at the Festival of Britain, and in a Flanders and Swann song, 'Surly Girls'. In fact something seemed to have been released in the national psyche. In the early 1950s, dressing up in school-girl uniforms was wildly popular at fancy-dress parties, rag weeks, hospital fund-raising drives and gang-shows. Of course it was all innocent fun. Or was it? Searle had drawn the girls in a deliberately unsexualized way. They were all unequivocally flat-chested, all deliberately greasy, spotty, un-made-up, bespectacled and recalcitrant – barely more physically attractive than Molesworth – but then... there *were* those stockings and suspender-belts. And they were invariably drawn with one leg showing a hint of garter. The St Trinian's phenomenon began to spiral out of Searle's control (despite his attempts to kill them off at around the time his daughter Kate herself started school). The innocent gym-slips inevitably began to seem not-so-innocent, or faux-innocent. Joan Collins dressed up as a St Trinian's schoolgirl for *Illustrated* magazine. The librarian of Richmond Public Library refused to stock *Back to the Slaughterhouse*, saying that 'there were other people with

different tastes, and those who studied it for various reasons.' And this was before the film comedies began. In the
filmic St Trinian's (*The Belles of St Trinian's*, 1954; *Blue Murder at St Trinian's*, 1957; *The Pure Hell of St Trinian's*, 1960;
and *The Great St Trinian's Train Robbery*, 1966), the older
girls were unashamedly alluring and sexually voracious;
girls on the make, the daughters of bookies and criminals,
on the dangerous cusp of womanhood, or, in fact, long
past it (one was even married), terrifying their male elders
with what they wished for but could not name.

Strangely enough, the real St Trinnean's did not become
known to the public until 1955, long after most of the cartoons and the first film had appeared. In September of that
year a notice appeared in the *Scotsman* advertising a school
reunion:

> St Trinian's Old Girls.
> A CEILIDH in the form of a COFFEE PARTY will
> be held on THURSDAY, 20th October 1955, at 8 o'clock
> at 16 GREAT STUART STREET, EDINBURGH, by
> kind permission of Miss C. FRASER LEE, to meet Miss
> BARBARA RENTON on her Appointment as Matron of
> Edinburgh Royal Infirmary. It is hoped that all Old Girls
> who can do so will come.

The typesetter, despite having been given the correct
spelling by the school, had mistakenly spelled it in the
Searle manner. The advertisement was spotted by the
Sunday Express, who tracked down and interviewed the
headmistress, now retired, Miss Fraser Lee, and ran a

splash piece on 'The awful truth about St Trinian's'. The article ran:

> White-haired, jolly Miss C. Fraser-Lee, the school's founder, threw back her head and laughed in her Great Stuart Street, Edinburgh flat.
>
> 'But I had no idea,' she said, 'that we were all going to be made some awful-looking people and that professors would afterwards look at me curiously and ask: 'Why did they call you Miss Umbridge?'
>
> 'Some of my old girls were most angry and wanted me to start a libel action. What fun that would have been!'

36

Performing Flea (1953)
PG Wodehouse

PERFORMING *Flea* is a collection of letters PG Wode-house wrote to his friend Bill Townend between 1920 and 1952. The book is all about the writing life. On every page there is some insight about how a writer handles his materials:

> What a sweat a novel is till you are sure of your charac-ters. And what a vital thing it is to have plenty of things for a major character to do. That is the test. If they aren't in a situation, characters can't be major characters, not even if you have the rest of the troupe talk their heads off about them.

All of this makes for fascinating reading – but the implica-tion of the title is rather surprising. Did Wodehouse really think of himself merely as a tiny entertainer in the smallest of literary arenas? This from the creator of Jeeves, Ukridge, Lord Emsworth, Mr Mulliner and Psmith?

The truth is that the title emerged from the most trau-matic year of Wodehouse's life.

On the outbreak of the Second World War, Wodehouse and his wife Ethel were living at Le Touquet, just south of Calais. Wodehouse was fifty-eight, and did not consider himself involved; his attitude to the war was almost entirely apolitical. Frances Donaldson, in her biography of him, reports a conversation in which Wodehouse said: 'If the Germans want to govern the world, why don't we just let them?' This was probably an extreme statement, since he was later on record as praising Churchill and saying that Germany was mad to take on the British, who would certainly win. But, presumably thinking himself invulnerable, he continued living at Le Touquet all through the 'phoney war' of 1939 and into 1940. Then, on May 22, 1940, the Germans arrived. The Wodehouses' car, bicycle, and the contents of their larder were requisitioned, and the Wodehouses were required to report regularly to the German authorities. Ethel described what happened next:

> One beautiful morning Plummie [i.e. Wodehouse] had just been down to report to Paris Plage. (I only reported on Saturdays.) I was arranging the lunch in the garden when he suddenly appeared and told me there was a German soldier in the hall waiting to take him to a concentration camp. He had only ten minutes to pack a suit case. I was nearly insane, couldn't find the keys of the room for the suit case, and Plum went off with a copy of Shakespeare, a pair of pyjamas, and a mutton chop.

Wodehouse was interned first in Loos Prison, then at a barracks in Liège, then at the Citadel at Huy, and finally at a camp at Tost, in Upper Silesia. This, despite what Ethel had said, was not a concentration camp – as we now understand the term – but an internment camp for enemy civilians. His imprisonment lasted just under a year, from July 1940 to the end of May 1941.

Wodehouse kept a notebook throughout, in which he recorded such thoughts as: 'I have never met an English-speaking German whom I didn't like instantly,' 'Prison brings out all that is best in us all' and 'It is amazing how this diet, which looks meagre, is really all one wants. One feels marvellous on it.' These remarks sound ironic, but Wodehouse actually meant them. He was extremely happy in camp, perhaps because it was in some ways rather like a public school. While there he wrote an entire novel, *Money in the Bank*, which he completed 'in pencil in a room where a hundred men were playing darts and ping-pong, with generally a lecture on Beowulf going on in the background'.

Enemy civilians were automatically released on turning sixty, and it was only a few weeks before Wodehouse's own automatic release that the Lagerführer at Tost, with whom Wodehouse was on cordial terms, suggested he make some radio broadcasts to America on camp life. Wodehouse had previously written a humorous article for the *Saturday Evening Post* called 'My War with Germany' – which the Lagerführer had read and appreciated – and he saw no harm in the idea. As he later said: 'I was feeling intensely happy in a mood that demanded expression and at the same time I was very grateful to all my American friends and very desirous of doing something to return their kindness in sending me letters and parcels.' There seems to have been no suggestion that the talks were a bargaining chip for his release, since he was going to be released anyway. But the fact is that he did get out a few weeks earlier than, in other circumstances, he might have done. This was probably the most damaging of all the facts later used against him. He arrived in Berlin on June 21, 1941 and recorded five talks. Their tone was one of light persiflage:

> There is a good deal to be said for any internment. It keeps you out of the saloon and gives you time to catch up with your reading. You also get a lot of sleep. The chief drawback is that it means your being away from home a good deal. It is not pleasant to think that by the time I see my Pekinese again, she will have completely forgotten me and will bite me to the bone – her invariable practice with strangers. And I feel that when I rejoin my wife, I had better take along a letter of introduction, just to be on the safe side.

Wodehouse's agreement to do the talks was foolish in the extreme. The crucial context, in June 1941, was that the USA was not yet involved in the war against Hitler. America was vacillating, and in propaganda terms Wodehouse's remarks, addressed, one should remember, to the Americans, were invaluable to Germany. They suggested, more in tone than anything else, that the Nazis were ultimately reasonable people who treated you fairly if firmly, and that life in a German prison camp, if looked at in the right spirit, could really be rather fun. The talks caused enormous offence in the USA, but they were picked up in Britain too, and this was where the real and permanent damage was done. The British press leapt on the story, particularly the *Mirror* journalist William Connor, who, writing under the name 'Cassandra', mounted a full-scale attack on Wodehouse:

> It appears that Mr. Wodehouse is to broadcast once a week to the United States. 'General chats, entirely non-political,' explained the Great Wag. He then went on: 'I am quite unable to work up any kind of belligerent feeling – really. Just as I'm about to feel belligerent about some country, I meet a decent sort of chap – we go out together and lose any fighting thoughts or feelings.'
>
> Mr Wodehouse is fortunate.
>
> He hasn't seen great areas of London, Coventry, Liverpool and other cities flattened by his Hunnish hosts. He hasn't heard the rattle of machine-gun fire as the gorillas of the Luftwaffe spray bullets at British seamen struggling in the water.

In 1941 there was still a possibility that Britain would be required to fight the Hun hand-to-hand on the beaches, and Wodehouse was badly out of touch with the national mood. Anthony Eden, as Foreign Secretary, was asked questions in Parliament, and said: 'His Majesty's government have seen with regret the report that Mr Wodehouse has lent his services to the German propaganda machine.' There were letters in the *Daily Telegraph*, some from fellow writers deploring his actions: AA Milne said that Wodehouse was behaving like a child 'hiding under the table' and that he did not deserve his 'enviable position above the battle' (for Milne's reasons for this attack see chapter 30). Cassandra followed up with more invective, broadcasting on the BBC: 'I have come to tell you tonight of the story of a rich man trying to make his last and greatest sale – that of his own country.' He accused Wodehouse of being a tax-dodger, a collaborator and a pawn of Goebbels. Perhaps the most unlikely of attackers was the playwright and Irish nationalist Sean O'Casey, who wrote a letter to the *Daily Telegraph* on July 8, 1941. His censure was more literary than political:

> It is amusing to read the various wails about the villainy of Wodehouse. The harm done to England's cause and to England's dignity is not the poor man's babble in Berlin, but the acceptance of him by a childish part of the people and the academic government of Oxford, dead from the chin up, as a person of any importance whatsoever in English humorous literature, or any literature at all. It is an ironic twist of retribution on those who banished Joyce and honoured Wodehouse.
>
> If England has any dignity left in the way of literature, she will forget for ever the pitiful antics of English Literature's performing flea. If Berlin thinks the poor fish great so much the better for us.

This notable example of kicking a man while he was down was the origin of the epithet Wodehouse used for his collection of letters. It is worth thinking about what this phrase 'performing flea' must have meant to Wodehouse. After the war, he tried to return to Britain, but his application was blocked. Instead he emigrated to the USA, never to return. The Cussen Report of 1945, a government investigation into the Berlin broadcasts, concluded that 'by lending his voice and personality to the German broadcasting station, Wodehouse did an act which was likely to assist the enemy,' though a note attached to it from the Director of Public Prosecutions said: 'There is not sufficient evidence to justify a prosecution of this man.' Wodehouse, uncertain how he stood – he never got to read the Cussen Report, which was only released in 1980, nor the note attached to it – stayed in Long Island, where he lived for a further thirty years, wrote around thirty-five more novels, and died in 1975. He was by the end of his life substantially rehabilitated, of course: his defenders eventually won the argument, especially as the crisis of war receded, presenting Wodehouse not as a quisling but as a political innocent who had blundered badly. But the broadcasts dogged him until the end. 'Performing flea' was an epithet of contempt, both political and literary, from very dark days, and a reminder for the rest of his life that he could never go home again. And he used it to title a book! This surely takes *sang-froid* to an entirely new level.

37

The Room (1957)
The Hothouse (1958)
Harold Pinter

THE Room was Pinter's first play, written in 1957. It exhibits the Pinter style *par excellence*, sprung as if fully-formed from the head of Samuel Beckett. Its characters speak in a way both banal and disturbing, ask questions that receive no answer or are answered immediately by the questioner, and constantly harp on things such as bacon, eggs, tea and cocoa:

> What about the rasher? Was it all right? It was a good
> one, I know, but not as good as the last lot I got in.

It is set in a single, imprisoning, claustrophobic room – the template for many of Pinter's later plays – in which the occupants, Rose, a soft-witted old woman, and Bert, an enormous silent lump, seem to wait with dread for some malign intruder. This personage finally arrives in the shape of Riley, who wishes to deliver a message but is savagely beaten.

Its origins lie in something that happened to the author one night in London in 1955. Pinter was at the time playing in rep in Colchester and went with an actress friend to a party in a house in Chelsea. He said that on entering a small room he encountered two men:

> The smaller of the two, a little barefooted man, was car-
> rying on a lively and rather literate conversation, and
> at the table next to him sat an enormous lorry driver.
> He had his cap on and never spoke a word. And all the
> while, as he talked, the little man was feeding the big
> man – cutting his bread, buttering it, and so on. Well,
> this image would never leave me… I told a friend,
> Henry Woolf, who was studying in the Drama Depart-
> ment of Bristol University, that I would write a play
> about them… It was *The Room*.

The image of the two men, one feeding the other, finds its parallel in the characters of Bert and Rose in *The Room*. And the room itself, of course, was crucial: without it Pinter would have had neither his title nor his setting. As he said solemnly in an interview with the BBC General Overseas Service in 1960:

> Two people in a room – I am dealing a great deal of
> the time with this image of two people in a room. The
> curtain goes up on the stage, and I see it as a very potent
> question: What is going to happen to these two people in
> a room? Is someone going to open the door and come in?

But there is something to add. The 'little man' was none other than Quentin Crisp. Crisp (1908-99) was the extraor-dinary violet-haired and be-hatted author of *The Naked Civil Servant*, an openly gay man in an era when homosexual acts were punishable by imprisonment. The house Pinter visited was the location of Crisp's bed-sit in Beaufort Street, Chelsea, where he lived with a gang of artists, actors and reprobates – 'a home for incorrigibles', as he put it, under the supervision of the landlady, a Miss Vereker, who had taken him in as 'one of the hazards of her dedication to humanity'. In another interview Pinter said:

> He welcomed us in, gave us a cup of tea, discussed philosophy and metaphysics, literature, the weather, crockery, fabrics. The little chap was dancing about cutting bread and butter, pouring tea and making bacon and eggs for this man who remained quite silent throughout the whole encounter... We left after about half an hour and I asked the woman what the little chap's name was and she said Quentin Crisp.

Crisp, it seems, stands at the very forefront of Harold Pinter's playwrighting career. One can only conclude that without Quentin Crisp there might have been no Harold Pinter.

The Hothouse is another very early Pinter play – written just after *The Birthday Party* and *A Slight Ache* in 1958 – though it was not performed until much later in 1980. Harold Pinter originally conceived of *The Hothouse* as a sixty-minute radio drama. He summarized it thus in 1958:

> The play is set in a psychological research centre.
> One department of this establishment is engaged in

conducting tests to determine reactions of the nervous
system to various stimuli. The subjects for these tests
are drawn from volunteers who are paid an hourly
rate for their services, in the interests of science.

This scenario substantially survived in the finished stage-
play, which is set in a government rest-home where the
patients are given electric shocks. The 'heat' of the hothouse suggests both the electric shocks and the sexual and
emotional arousal of both torturers and tortured.

But the theme and title came from Pinter's own turn in
the hot-seat in 1954, when he submitted himself to medical
experiments for cash. He recalled to Michael Billington:

> I went along in 1954 to the Maudsley Hospital in
> London, as a guinea-pig. They were offering ten bob
> or something for guinea-pigs and I needed the money
> desperately. I read a bona fide advertisement and went
> along. It was all above board, as it seemed. Nurses and
> doctors all in white. They tested my blood-pressure first.
> Perfectly all right. I was put in a room with electrodes.
> They said, 'Just sit there for a while and relax.' I'd no
> idea what was going to happen. Suddenly there was a
> most appalling noise through the earphones and I nearly
> jumped through the roof. I felt my heart go...BANG! The
> noise lasted a few seconds and then was switched off.
> The doctor came in grinning and said, 'Well, that really
> gave you a start, didn't it?' I said, 'It certainly did.' And
> they said, 'Thanks very much.' There was no interroga-
> tion, as in the play, but it left a deep impression on me. I
> couldn't forget the experience. I was trembling all over.
> And I would have been in such a vulnerable position if

they had started to ask me questions. Later I asked them
what it was all about and they said they were testing
levels of reaction. That mystified me. Who exactly were
they going to give this kind of shock-treatment to? Anyway, *The Hothouse* was kicked off by that experience.

In the play a similar thing happens to the earnest and inof-
fensive Lamb. He is asked to help with 'some little tests',
which involve him having electrodes attached to his wrists
and his head covered by earphones. The experimenters
soothe him, telling him to relax, and then suddenly:

> LAMB jolts rigid, his hands go to his earphones, he is
> propelled from the chair, falls to his knees, twisting from
> side to side, still clutching his earphones, emitting high-
> pitched cries.

It's clear that there are serious themes in *The Hothouse*, as in
The Birthday Party, where Goldberg and McCann's interroga-
tion of Stanley Webber, and their membership of a shadowy
organization, are suggestive of the Gestapo. *The Hothouse* also
seems to prefigure more political pieces such as *One for the
Road* and *Mountain Language*. Pinter was obviously thinking
of the use of science as torture: 'I would have been in such a
vulnerable position if they had started to ask me questions.'
The element of sexual aggression is very much to the fore,
dealing as it does with doctors who seduce, impregnate and
murder their patients. It's intriguing that Pinter delayed public performance for twenty-two years. Perhaps he still felt too
close to his traumatic experience at the Maudsley.

38

Goldfinger (1959)
Ian Fleming

IT began on a golf course.

In the 1950s, Ian Fleming's regular golfing partner was a businessman called John Blackwell. One day, at the St George's Golf Club in Sandwich, Blackwell mentioned to Fleming that his cousin's husband was the architect Ernö Goldfinger. Fleming liked the name 'Goldfinger' and thought he might be able to use it: he was always on the look-out for new or unusual names, and had given several of his previous characters the names of real people (and in fact in the final text of *Goldfinger* he used John Blackwell's name for a minor character, a 'pleasant-spoken Import and Export merchant').

In the book, Auric (rather than Ernö) Goldfinger is a Russian agent working for the underground organization SMERSH. His mission is to capture the West's gold stocks by robbing Fort Knox and exporting one billion dollars' worth of bullion to the Soviet Union, so precipitating an economic crisis. His villainy does not end there. He loves gold to the point of insanity, prefers his women to be decorated all over in gold paint before he has sex with them, and at one point executes an unfaithful secretary by leaving her to languish in this paint until her blocked pores cause her to suffocate (actually an impossible method of execution, though the victim might eventually die of heatstroke). At one point there is a golf match between Bond and Auric Goldfinger (who cheats, being foreign), perhaps as a nod to the original moment of titular inspiration on the golf course. *Goldfinger* is a typical James Bond romp, full of sexually voracious females with silly names, joke thermonuclear warheads, flash gadgets and casual racism. Auric Goldfinger is assumed to be Jewish and is introduced as follows: 'You won't believe it, but he's a Britisher. Domiciled in Nassau. You'd think he'd be a Jew from the name, but he doesn't look it.'

Fleming might have thought that no-one would notice his appropriation of the name, but he was mistaken. Ern☐ Goldfinger was one of post-war Britain's most prominent architects and designers, a leader of the so-called 'Brutalist'[44] movement. A Jewish-Hungarian émigré, he was a highly flamboyant character with a love of fast cars, cigars and young women, and thought by some to be rather a bully: there were stories that he was given to frog-marching uncooperative clients out of his offices. Some time before publication he got wind of the book and asked his solicitors to contact Fleming's publisher, Jonathan Cape, for an explanation. Jonathan Cape sent a pre-publication copy of

---

44 Goldfinger always denied that he had anything to do with the 'Brutalist' movement, which is not in itself surprising: the label was originally pejorative. Brutalism was distinguished by rectlilinear forms often in unadorned cast concrete.

the novel to Goldfinger so that he could check it for libel. This was not difficult to spot. Both the real and the fictional Goldfinger exhibited Communistic tendencies (Ernö was a lifelong Marxist and had designed the *Daily Worker* building); in both cases there was the Jewish connection; a third similarity was a love of fast cars. Driving while a Jewish Communist was not, of course, a crime, or libellous in itself, but the fact that the fictional Goldfinger was also a murdering traitorous pervert was enough to give Ernö a good case for a libel suit if he so chose. He decided to sue.

Jonathan Cape behaved as sensible publishers do. They soothed the architect and suggested a number of concessions. They would not go as far as removing Goldfinger's name from the jacket, but they would make sure that whenever it was mentioned in the text of the book it would be in the full form 'Auric Goldfinger', thus detaching the villain from his nominal model. There would also be the standard disclaimer at the front of the book: 'The characters in this book are all fictional and no reference is intended to any person, alive or dead.' Ernö would be sent six copies of the novel with the author's compliments, and the publishers would pay all costs of the legal action incurred so far. Rather generously, Ernö agreed, and took no further action.

Fleming, however, was not pleased. It was a clash of two egos of rather similar size and shape. Fleming (also a womanizer, fast-car lover, occasional bully[45], etc.) considered getting his revenge by renaming the villain

---

[45] Fleming's wife Ann once wrote to him: 'It's very lonely not to be beaten and shouted at every five minutes.'

'Goldprick' and inserting a slip into all the books explaining why this had had to be done: eventually he cooled off and the book went to press with the provisos Goldfinger's solicitors had stipulated.

Fleming might have taken comfort from the fact that the huge success of the book and later the 1964 film produced some minor inconveniences for Ern□. As Nigel Warburton reports in his biography of Goldfinger, the architect was often called late at night by people singing the song from the film ('Gold... FINGer...') or impersonating Sean Connery. Finally Goldfinger began to enjoy his alter ego's infamy. He never had to repeat his name at parties. And in his office he kept prominently displayed one of his free first-edition copies of the novel.

Oddly enough Ern□ Goldfinger inspired another literary creation. This time the book concerned did not bear his name but drew inspiration from his career. It was JG Ballard's *High Rise* of 1975, which was almost certainly instigated by the furore associated with Goldfinger's Trellick Tower, a building completed a couple of years earlier. Trellick Tower was the most notorious of Britain's high-rise residential blocks, and was given the tabloid nickname 'The Tower of Terror'. The particular scale of Trellick Tower – the tallest of the Goldfinger buildings at thirty-one storeys – made it a symbolic scapegoat for all the perceived disadvantages of high-rise living: anonymity, lack of surveillance, multiple escape routes for criminals. In Ballard's *High Rise*, a tower block descends into anarchy as the inhabitants first retreat from one another, and then, as social conditions worsen, emerge with rudimentary weapons to shed one another's blood: the high-rise dwelling becomes, as Ballard put it, 'an environment built not for man, but for man's absence'. But fortunes improved for the real Trellick Tower, and by the turn of the century its flats were among the most sought-after in London – two-bedroom properties there now sell for £422,000, and it is a Grade II star listed building, which means it can never be demolished. It is certainly the best-known Brutalist high-rise in Britain, and among the most famous in Europe. *High Rise*, then, like many of Ballard's other apocalypses (*The Drowned World*, *The Burning World*), seems, with the advantage of hindsight, more valuable as an expression of Ballard's literary psychology than as social commentary or 'prophecy' in any conventional sense.

But the fact that Ballard attached himself to Ernő Gold-finger was a strange coincidence. What was it about this man? Goldfinger tended to accrue, as if by magnetism, a completely undeserved reputation for villainy.

39

Interlude 3:
La Disparition by Georges Perec
Eunoia by Christian Bök
Adventures in Capitalism by Toby Litt
Ladle Rat Rotten Hut by Howard L Chace
Never Again by Doug Nufer
Green Eggs and Ham by Dr Seuss

THE titles above are all titles tortured. Each is in some way constrained, and announces a work that is similarly constrained.

Constrained writing adopts restrictions on what is or is not permitted in the text. These constraints then serve to generate the text. Devices of constraint are in fact sometimes called 'generative devices' because of their suggestive power.

The twentieth century was especially good for constrained writing, due to the influence of a French movement known as 'Oulipo' (for the *Ouvroir de Littérature Potentielle*, or Workshop of Potential Literature). Founded by a group of writers and mathematicians in

1960, Oulipo was interested in reviving ancient literary forms and creating new ones, often with self-imposed restrictions. Oulipo loved bondage. As Marcel Bénabou, Oulipo's Definitely Provisional Secretary put it, charting his (fictive) literary career in his book *Why I Have Not Written Any of My Books* (1986): 'The absence of any constraint, of any form, of any rule, would have led me to the very place I did not want to go: the lukewarm desert of narcissism and self-indulgence.'

Perhaps the best-known category of constrained writing is the lipogram. Lipogrammatic texts create mini-voids in language by barring certain letters – usually the commonest letters, such as 'e'. Georges Perec, the quintessential Oulipo practitioner, wrote numerous quirky books, but his lipogrammatic novel *La Disparition* (1969) is perhaps his most famous.[46] This omits the letter 'e' throughout (including in the title), and was wittily translated by Gilbert Adair as *A Void*. The plot concerns a group of people who are hunting an absent friend, Anton Vowl. The characters comment throughout on the strange constraint they seem to be toiling under, though of course without being able to refer to the very thing that is missing. And the absence of 'e' seems to signify something else: Perec was Jewish, and his parents both died in the Second World War, his father in battle, his

---

[46] Lipograms are not restricted to the French. *Gadsby* (1939) by Ernest Wright, another lipogrammatic novel omitting the letter 'e', predated *La Disparition* by thirty years. Another distinguished effort is Mark Dunn's *Ella Minnow Pea* (2001), which progressively dispenses with all the letters of the alphabet. Nor are lipograms in fact particularly modern: they were popular as long ago as the ancient Greeks. Nestor wrote a lipogrammatic *Iliad*; Tryphiodorus did the same with the *Odyssey*; Lope de Vega is said to have written five lipogrammatic novels. The lipogram virus turns up too in ancient Persian writings. There is a story that the Sufi poet Jami was once approached by a colleague who wished to show him a poem in which the letter 'aleph' had been omitted. Jami sarcastically told him: 'You can do a better thing yet; take away all the letters from every word you have written.'

mother in Auschwitz. He was brought up as an orphan by his aunt and uncle. Perec in his novel is unable to say '*mère*' or '*père*' or '*famille*': the loss of a letter seems to stand in for greater losses, and things unspoken, or unspeakable.

A novel with similar stylistic concerns is Christian Bök's surprise bestseller of 2001, *Eunoia*, which constrains itself not by excluding single letters but by permitting only one vowel per chapter. It took seven years to write. The title *Eunoia*, which contains all the vowels once, means 'beautiful thinking'. Thus the third chapter is written using only the vowel 'i':

> Hiking in British districts, I picnic in virgin firths, grinning in mirth with misfit whims, smiling if I find birch twigs, smirking if I find mint sprigs.

In the final chapter only 'u' is permitted.

> Gulls churr: ululu, ululu. Ducks cluck. Bulls plus bucks run thru buckbrush; thus dun burrs clutch fur tufts. Ursus cubs plus Lupus pups hunt skunks.

Toby Litt is another writer in English who employs constraints. These are most visibly attached to his titles: they all begin with sequential letters of the alphabet. As of 2010, in order of publication, they are *Adventures in Capitalism*, *Beatniks*, *Corpsing*, *deadkidsongs*, *Exhibitionism*, *Finding Myself*, *Ghost Story*, *Hospital*, *I play the drums in a band called okay*, *Journey into Space*, *King Death* and *Life-Like*. The sequence was planned from the beginning. Litt said in an interview:

'I knew whilst writing *Adventures* that it was – if I ever got it published – the start of an alphabetical cycle. One of the other students in my year was Richard Beard, an English Oulipian. He wrote according to constraints, and several of the stories in *Adventures* had constraints. The alphabetical titles was a similar idea.'

Constrained writing tends to attract intellectuals. Consider the case of Howard L Chace, an American Professor of Romance Languages, who in 1940 wrote the children's classic *Ladle Rat Rotten Hut*. This was 'Little Red Riding Hood' as it had never been seen or heard before: the generative device consisted of 'homophonic transformation', or of finding a similar sounding English word (or group of words) for every word (or group of words) in a familiar story. The result was like listening to a Dutchman speaking from a parallel dimension:

> Wants pawn term dare worsted ladle gull hoe lift wetter
> murder inner ladle cordage honor itch offer lodge, dock
> florist. Disk ladle gull orphan worry putty ladle rat cluck
> wetter ladle rat hut, an fur disk raisin pimple colder
> Ladle Rat Rotten Hut.

Ladle Rat Rotten Hut goes off to meet her groin-murder but is waylayed by an anomalous woof. Chace's retold tale became a media sensation, being featured on radio and television and becoming a bedtime favourite for a generation of children (it was first published in 1956 in Chace's collection *Anguish Languish*, which also included the fairy stories 'Guilty Looks Enter Tree Beers', the nursery rhyme

'Sinker Sucker Socks Pants' and the songs 'Hive Ban Walking Honor Roil Rut' and 'Hurl, Hurl, Door Gong's Oil Hair').

The novel *Never Again* (2004) by Doug Nufer (whose name sounds like it has been constrained in some unidentifiable way) also has a title that reflects its self-imposed limitations: no word is ever to be repeated throughout the text. *Never Again* tells the story of a reformed gambler who is determined not to re-commit his past mistakes, and tries to achieve this by never repeating any action or utterance. It begins:

> When the racetrack closed forever I had to get a job.
> Want ads made wonderlands, founding systems barely
> imagined. Adventure's imperative ruled nothing could
> repeat.

Finally, in this short survey of constrained titles, it would be wrong to omit one of the great classics of limitation. Severely academic, riotously funny, unexpectedly moving and enormously successful: what else other than *Green Eggs and Ham* (1960) by Dr Seuss? *Green Eggs and Ham* followed the success of *The Cat in the Hat*, which used a limited lexicon of 236 words to encourage very young children to read. Seuss's publisher at Random House, Bennett Cerf, bet him $50 that he could not write a book using a lexicon of only 50 words. Seuss, after much labour, produced *Green Eggs and Ham*, in which Sam-I-Am tries to persuade his friend to eat this dish in various locations (in a house, with a mouse, on a boat, with a goat), and finally succeeds – to his friend's great surprise and pleasure. The *New Yorker* said that Seuss could 'play so many tunes on his simplified keyboard that, reading him, one is hardly aware that there *are* more than fifty words.' The title itself is strangely inverted: the American expression is 'ham and eggs', not 'eggs and ham', and it is the inversion that opens up the charmed world the reader enters. But in early drafts it *was* 'Green ham and eggs'. This early manuscript fragment shows Seuss tussling with his constrained medium:

> I do not like them
> On a tree
> Green ham and eggs
> On a green green tree
> I do not like you
> Sam I am
> Your tree, your eggs
> Your car, your ham.

Seuss must have felt that there were no useful rhymes for 'eggs' that could be included in a limited lexicon of 50 words. The order was reversed to give the magically counter-familiar 'green eggs and ham'.

Bennett Cerf claimed Seuss was a genius, but Seuss responded: 'If I'm a genius, why do I have to work so hard? I know my stuff looks like it was all rattled off in 28 seconds, but every word is a struggle and every sentence is like the pangs of birth.'

Other constrained writers would surely sympathize.

40

The Worm and the Ring (1961)
Anthony Burgess

THE title of this novel by Burgess is rather odd. There is no mention in the book of either worms or rings, and the plot, set in a grammar school (Burgess was for several years a schoolteacher at Banbury near Oxford), is about the theft of a diary. Then one realizes – or is told by some kindly person – that the whole book is in fact a re-telling, on one level, of the Wagnerian ring cycle. It opens with Albert Rich (the dwarf Alberich in the ring cycle), a schoolboy, pursuing some giggling schoolgirls (three Rhine-maidens). Then it introduces the headmaster Woolton (Wotan, the chief of the Gods) and his wife Frederica (Fricka, the consort of Wotan). There is another character called Lodge (Loge, or Loki, god of fire), a girl called Linda (Woglinde, one of the Rhine-maidens), and a pub called 'the Dragon' ('worm' being an archaic word for dragon). The stolen diary stands in for the stolen ring. As a title, then, *The Worm and the Ring* is comprehensible at this Wagnerian altitude. But just to complicate matters, Burgess claimed in his memoir *Little Wilson and Big God* that it also echoed a more modern mythic structure, that of Catholic Christianity:

> It was the real meaning of the title *The Worm and the Ring*. Christopher Howarth the hero is no true Siegfried. He is a renegade Catholic married to a devout daughter of the Church who, suffering from Lynne's [Burgess's wife's] ailment of dysmenorrhoea, forbids marital sex. They have a son who may be regarded as the imaginary fulfillment of Lynne's own thwarted pregnancy. While Howarth is fornicating with Hilda in the school library, instead of patrolling the playground as master on duty, the son climbs on to a roof to retrieve a ball thrown there, falls on to spiked railings (like the Alec Mitchell of my youth) and dies in agony. The father's guilt is so extreme as to be near-comic. He crawls like a worm; he has betrayed not merely the ring of marriage but the twin golden rounds of social and religious responsibility.

It's all very interesting: a title that simultaneously allegorizes pagan *and* Christian myth, for a novel in which disguised gods and heroes play out Catholic dramas of betrayal, guilt and atonement. Burgess seems to have thought, at least in his early period, that the duty of the novelist was to weave a rich vein of arcane symbolism into his work, accessible only to the initiated. He was influenced in this belief by two things: musicology and James Joyce.

Burgess was a composer before he was a novelist. As a schoolboy he composed a Prelude and Fugue in D Minor in the style of Bach, and went on to write several symphonies (the first in E: he remembered that 'the labour of copying those four sharps over and over was very exhausting'), as well as operas, partitas, sonatas, a Passacaglia for Orchestra, and much else. Burgess, then, emerged into the world of novel-making from a comparatively unusual direction, and found the novel, as a discipline, rather less demanding than the symphony. He said in his memoir:

> In a symphony many strands conjoined, in the same instant, to make a statement; in a novel all you had was a single line of monody. The ease with which dialogue could be written seemed grossly unfair. This was not art as I had known it. It seemed cheating not to be able to give the reader chords and counterpoint. It was like pretending that there could be such a thing as a concerto for unaccompanied flute.

It was Joyce who showed him the way round the problem of the nugatory novel:

> My notion of giving the reader his money's worth was to throw difficult words and neologisms at him, to make the syntax involuted. Anything, in fact, to give the impression of a musicalisation of prose. I saw that that was what Joyce had really been trying to do in *Finnegans Wake* – clotting words into chords, presenting several stories simultaneously in an effect of counterpoint. I was not trying to emulate *Finnegans Wake* – which had closed gates rather than opened them – but I felt that *Ulysses* had still plenty to teach to a musician who was turning to fiction.

Joyce in *Ulysses* had used the structure of the *Odyssey* for the eighteen 'episodes' of his book. Now Burgess could do the same. His first attempt at a novel was *A Vision of Battlements* (written in 1953 and published in 1965). *A Vision of Battlements* was modelled on *Ulysses*, except that where *Ulysses* took its structure from Homer's *Odyssey*, *A Vision of Battlements* used Vergil's *Aeneid*. The hero of the novel is one Richard Ennis (Ennis corresponding to Aeneas, the warrior-hero of the *Aeneid*), a member of the AVCC, or Army Vocational and Cultural Corps, jokingly referred to as the Arma Virumque Cano Corps (*Arma virumque cano*, 'Of arms and the man I sing', being the first three words of the *Aeneid*). He becomes sexually entangled with a Dido-figure called Concepcion, who is being pursued by a businessman named Barasi (an anagram of Iarbas, Dido's suitor in the *Aeneid*). With touching bathos Burgess revealed that the title had actually been filched from a copy of *The Illustrated Family Doctor*, which spoke of the symptoms of migraine: 'Warning of an attack may be given by tingling sensations in the limbs, impairment of vision, flashing lights, a vision of battlements, noises in the ears, mental depression or other phenomena.' *The Worm and the Ring* was his second novel and did the same thing with the Ring cycle.

Burgess never quite outgrew this compulsion to provide his books with hidden structures, though it became more attenuated as his career progressed. *Napoleon Symphony* (1974), an attempt to re-cast Beethoven's *Eroica* symphony as a novel, and *Mozart and the Wolf Gang* (1991) which mirrors the structure of Mozart's Symphony No.40, exhibit the tendency, and it is there too in his most famous book, *A Clockwork Orange*.[47] But finally he expressed doubts as to whether what was appropriate in a musical composition was also appropriate in a novel. He wrote in *Little Wilson and Big God* that *A Vision of Battlements* had 'a lack of solidity in the intention':

> Ennis does his best to follow in the path of Aeneas, but the signposts are ambiguous. [...] The Vergilian references are all too, so to speak, appliqué. 'Here's the Hampton Court maze, where we got lost on our honeymoon... And here's the last photograph my dear son had taken... died in training. He was just getting his wings. My husband, you see, had been in the Flying Corps.' If anyone recognizes Daedalus and Icarus here, how far does it help the story?

---

47 As Burgess made clear in a 1986 essay, 'A Clockwork Orange Resucked', each of the three parts of *A Clockwork Orange* has seven chapters, adding up to twenty-one in all, twenty-one being the age at which a young person achieves adult maturity: Burgess's wranglings over the famously-deleted final chapter (deleted in the American edition, retained in the English) were partly to do with his fears that if the last chapter were pruned, the symmetry would be destroyed.

41

The Whitsun Weddings (1964)
High Windows (1974)
Philip Larkin

THE Whitsun Weddings is a title that can be given a precise date. Inspiration struck on May 28, 1955 (Whit Saturday) as Larkin took the train from Hull to London. He said in an interview with Melvyn Bragg on *The South Bank Show* in 1981:

> I caught a very slow train that stopped at every station and I hadn't realized that, of course, this was the train that all the wedding couples would get on and go to London for their honeymoon[;] it was an eye-opener to me. Every part was different but the same somehow. They all looked different but they were all doing the same things and sort of feeling the same things. I suppose the train stopped at about four, five, six stations between Hull and London and there was a sense of gathering emotional momentum. Every time you stopped fresh emotion climbed aboard. And finally between Peterborough and London when you hurtle on, you felt the whole thing was being aimed like a bullet –

at the heart of things, you know. All this fresh, open life.
Incredible experience. I've never forgotten it.

The experience became the poem 'The Whitsun Weddings', which gave its name to the title of Larkin's third collection of poetry – which happened to be the collection that cemented his reputation.

> That Whitsun, I was late getting away:
>   Not till about
> One-twenty on the sunlit Saturday
> Did my three-quarters-empty train pull out,
> All windows down, all cushions hot, all sense
> Of being in a hurry gone.

The poem is roughly consonant in tone with the *South Bank Show* interview above. Its mood is also one of 'fresh emotion' and optimism: the train carriages are charged with burgeoning life and potential, 'ready to be loosed with all the power / that being changed can give.' Not even the 'uncles shouting smut', the 'fathers with broad belts under their suits', and the girls staring 'at a religious wounding' can dampen the poet's mood of quiet celebration. Optimism, new beginnings, 'fresh, open life' – not the most characteristic Larkin voice. And three weeks after completing the poem (on October 18, 1957, after a more-than-two-year struggle through dozens of drafts) he wrote what may be considered a companion-piece to 'The Whitsun Weddings'. This is 'Self's the Man', a poem with a less sanguine view of matrimony:

Oh, no-one can deny
That Arnold is less selfish than I.
He married a woman to stop her getting away
Now she's there all day...

It is a portrait of stultifying marital servitude. Tellingly, 'Self's the Man' appears immediately after 'The Whitsun Weddings' in the collection. 'The Whitsun Weddings' seems to be there to represent one sort of Larkin, a nice Larkin, perhaps, a Larkin wishing to show himself capable of being moved by ordinary human connections (as in 'An Arundel Tomb' or 'Show Saturday'). 'Self's the Man', by immediate contrast, presents a nasty Larkin, a more realist, misogynist and misanthropist Larkin, the Larkin Tom Paulin inveighed against.[48] And if one had to choose which of these two Larkins now dominates the public mind, one would have to choose the nasty Larkin, partly because the nice Larkin sometimes fails to convince: he muses in 'The Whitsun Weddings', for example, that 'none / Thought of the others they would never meet / Or how their lives would all contain this hour.' Really? Could none of these couples be expected to notice they were all sharing the same train? Isn't the thirty-two-year-old Larkin just a little too condescending, patrician here? 'Self's the Man', a brutal squib, seems by contrast to give us the stripped-away Larkin voice, the one that will wear the decades. Larkin's best-known poem, after all, is undoubtedly the nasty 'This Be the Verse', with its first line stating the irrevocable destiny of all honeymoon couples – to become parents:

---

48 'Larkin's snarl, his populism and his calculated philistinism all speak for Tebbit's England and for that gnarled and angry puritanism which is so deeply ingrained in the culture.' (*Times Literary Supplement*, July 1990)

They fuck you up, your mum and dad.

Larkin's last collection again takes its title again from one of its major poems, 'High Windows', which begins:

> When I see a couple of kids
> And guess he's fucking her and she's
> Taking pills or wearing a diaphragm,
> I know this is paradise...

The poet thinks of his own youth, wondering whether anyone envied him his freedom then (*'That'll be the life; / No God any more, or sweating in the dark / About hell and that'*), and then arrives at an unexpected, mystical conclusion:

> Rather than words comes the thought of high windows:
> The sun-comprehending glass,
> And beyond it, the deep blue air, that shows
> Nothing, and is nowhere, and is endless.

But high windows where? In a cathedral perhaps? A skyscraper? What do the high windows represent? There are several possible influences. Larkin might have been making reference to a novel by Raymond Chandler, *The High Window* of 1942; he would presumably have enjoyed employing Chandler in such a capacity. But there is also a biographical connection. From 1956 to 1974, while working at the Brynmor Jones library at Hull University, Larkin lived in a flat overlooking Pearson Park, Hull. It was a top floor flat, giving him a good view of the park. It was here that he wrote *High Windows*, and here that he could sit 'Under a lamp, hearing the noise of wind, / And looking out to see the moon thinned / To an air-sharpened blade' (*'Vers de Société'*). The 'high windows', in this reading, seem to stand for the solitary life, the rejection of envy, a life carved out in defiance of what the worlds of sensuality or bogus spirituality have to offer. This is one biographical possibility. Another concerns his working life. Larkin's offices at the Brynmor Jones library also had a commanding view, this time over the concourse where the students would walk in from the main road to the lecture halls and student union. According to his secretary, one of Mr Larkin's favourite recreations was to observe from this office, through an ever-warm spy-glass, the female students as they walked beneath him ('When I see a couple of kids...') He called the attractive ones his 'honeys'. Is the dirty beginning of the poem therefore tied to a subtextual dirty end?[49] Of course this is an absurdly literal way of looking at it: the high windows are not supposed to represent any real vantage-point, and are even, in the poem, presented 'rather than words', as if conventional metaphor, with its aim of corresponding in some way to reality, is inadequate. And yet the idea of high windows, and of looking down, and the intrusion of a seemingly unrelated visionary moment at the

---

[49] The odd fact is that in the first drafts, in the version of March 1965, the last stanza reads:

Rather than words comes the thought of high windows:
The sun pouring through plain glass
And beyond them deep blue air that shows
Nothing, and nowhere, and is endless.

and fucking piss.

This should probably not over-influence our reading of the poem.

conclusion of a very concrete poem ('fucking', 'diaphragm', 'sweating in the dark') crops up again, a few poems later in the collection. The poem is 'Money':

> Quarterly, is it, money reproaches me:
>> 'Why do you let me lie here wastefully?
> I am all you never had of goods and sex.
>> You could get them still by writing a few cheques.'

The focus is on the basics of life, on 'goods and sex'. As the poem develops, the idea is elaborated: money is there to be used rather than hoarded. And then, as in 'High Windows', the last stanza takes a surprising turn:

> I listen to money singing. It's like looking down
>> From long french windows at a provincial town,
> The slums, the canal, the churches ornate and mad
>> In the evening sun. It is intensely sad.

Again the image arrives out of the blue. Again we see Larkin, Rapunzel-like, looking down from his high window. As in 'High Windows', the image does not resolve the poem's argument but, Zen-like, steps outside the argument to present us with something new, a picture of a detached observer perched in some eyrie or niche above the rest of humanity, seeking answers but finding none. Something very personal seems to be going on here, something to do with always living a storey above everyone else. Perhaps the biographical explanations are correct after all.

42

Accidental Death of an Anarchist (1970)
Dario Fo

ON December 12, 1969, at four-thirty in the afternoon, a bomb exploded at the National Agricultural Bank in the Piazza Fontana, Milan, killing 17 people and injuring scores more. Several anarchists were immediately arrested, including a ballet dancer, Pietro Valpreda (who spent three years in jail but was eventually released and exonerated) and Giuseppe Pinelli, a 41-year-old railway worker. Pinelli spent three days in police custody in Milan, but on the night of December 15 he plummeted from the fourth-storey window of the police headquarters where he was (illegally) being held. According to the testimony of police officers in the room with him at the time, he went to the window of his own volition and threw himself out of it with 'a cat-like leap'. He was pronounced dead at the scene. Clearly, the police said, it was suicide. Police chief Marcello Guida went further: it was proof of his guilt, since no innocent man would behave in such a way.

However there were witnesses to the defenestration of Giuseppe Pinelli. One journalist, below in the street, said that he had been surprised to see a confusion at the window and had thought: 'What the hell are they doing up there? Why are they throwing a big box out of the window?' One disturbing detail was that Pinelli seemed to have no injuries to his hands, the normal result of a man falling to his death and instinctively holding out his hands to cushion the impact. Was he therefore already unconscious or dead?

As the days and weeks dragged by, no charges were brought against the police. The climate of the time was extremely febrile. The Piazza Fontana bombing had taken place at a time of worker's demonstrations and strikes – the so-called 'Hot Autumn'. After the bombing, the far right called for a clampdown, saying that the left – who they blamed for the bombing and for other similar attacks – were an 'irresponsible and subversive minority' who were seeking to 'paralyse public life'. The police, in such a climate, were untouchable. Any revelation of guilt in police ranks for the death of Pinelli would have been national suicide, as a former prime minister, Ferruccio Parri, later made clear: 'The judiciary is insisting on creating a verdict which saves the police, because the police are the state.' The final verdict on the Pinelli affair was one of 'accidental death'.

This, then, was the event that inspired Dario Fo's play, *Morte accidentale d'un anarchico*, or *Accidental Death of an Anarchist*. There is no mention of Pinelli in the play. The main characters instead are one Inspector Bertozzo and an unnamed 'Maniac' who infiltrates the police headquarters and impersonates a visiting judge. 'The Maniac' makes Fo's opinion clear on the real motives behind the bank atrocity:

> The main intention behind the massacre of innocent people in the bank bombing had been to bury the trade union struggles of the 'Hot Autumn' and to create a climate of tension so that the average citizen would be so disgusted and angry at the level of political violence and subversion that they would start calling for the intervention of a strong state!

Once most of the anarchists had been released, attention did at last switch to the far right. Several trials of far-right group members – particularly linked to the neofascist group *Ordine Nuovo* – were held. Convictions were at first obtained, but then overthrown on appeal. In 2004, thirty-five years after the Piazza Fontana bombing, a court found that *Ordine Nuovo* members Franco Freda and Giovanni Ventura were guilty of the bombing but could not be convicted because they had already been tried once and acquitted.

Such is the story of *Accidental Death of an Anarchist*. The nicely-judged irony of the title goes some way to explaining why Fo won the Nobel Prize: it is not *Murder of an Anarchist* but *Accidental Death of an Anarchist*, an ironic echo of the verdict handed down after Pinelli's 'cat-like leap'.

What is perhaps rather surprising is that any English-speaking reader has heard of this play at all. Why would a play drawing on Italian political events become a smash hit, running for one and a half years? Why was Dario Fo so popular here?[50]

The context, of course, was Thatcherism and the wilderness years for the left in Britain. British politics was polarized to an extent now difficult to remember, and the left needed a drama reflecting its concerns. It already had figures such as Tom Stoppard (*Dogg's Hamlet, Cahoot's Macbeth*) and Caryl Churchill (*Cloud Nine, Top Girls*), and there were revivals of Brecht's *Mother Courage* and *Good Woman of Szechuan*, but there was a hunger for more. Fo was unimpeachably left-wing, a man who (according to the critic Ros Asquith) 'happily combined the Marxism of both Harpo and Karl while remaining mercifully independent of the Kremlin line'. When it opened in 1979 at the Half Moon Theatre, *Accidental Death of an Anarchist* was also explicitly linked with the murder of the teacher Blair Peach (who had died, some said, at the hands of the police[51]). But who were the people actually going to the theatre? Perhaps not the kind of audience Fo usually courted or even wanted. Generally Fo preferred to distance himself from bourgeois theatreland, playing instead to mass audiences in sports stadia and factories, or taking his work on the road to communist Romania or apartheid South Africa. In Britain something rather different happened. Fo was gentrified. The audiences that flocked to see Fo were not

---

50 At one point in 1981, three of Fo's plays, *Accidental Death of an Anarchist, Can't Pay, Won't Pay* and *One Woman Plays* were running simultaneously, at the Albery, Criterion and National Theatres respectively.

51 An investigation in 2010, thirty-one years later, attached grave suspicion to a police officer of the Special Patrol Group identified only as Officer E.

the oppressed masses but middle-class, left-leaning, play-going Londoners. Fo's political theatre became the badge of socialism for the frustrated bourgeoisie at a time when the working classes were all voting for Mrs T.

43

John Thomas and Lady Jane (1972)
DH Lawrence

DH Lawrence produced three full-length versions of *Lady Chatterley's Lover* between 1925 and 1928. Frieda Lawrence described her husband's working habits at this time, while they were living at the Villa Mirenda, in the hills above Florence:

> It was an enchanting place where Lawrence went to write every day, especially in Spring. He had to walk a little way by the olive trees to get to his umbrella pine. Thyme and mint tufts grew along the path and purple anemones and wild gladioli and carpets of violets and myrtle shrubs. White, calm oxen were ploughing.
>
> There he would sit, almost motionless except for his swift writing. He would be so still that the lizards would run over him and the birds hop close around him. An occasional hunter would start at this silent figure.

In the first version the gamekeeper is called Parkin (rather than, as in the final version, Mellors), and the decision to make him a gamekeeper, with a house in the woods, may owe something to this setting in the umbrella pinewood. All the main plot elements are there in the first version: Clifford, an aristocratic mine-owner, has been injured in the war and is paralyzed from the waist down; Connie, his wife, is drawn into an affair with a lower-class man and achieves a new awareness of her physical self. Written in a few weeks and finished by early December 1926, this version exists as a separate manuscript, and was first published in 1944 as *The First Lady Chatterley*, a title chosen by Frieda Lawrence. Frieda herself preferred this version (as have many other readers), and said of it: '*The First Lady Chatterley* he wrote as she came out of him, out of his own immediate self. In the third version he was also aware of his contemporaries' minds.'

Immediately Lawrence had finished it, he began revising. The revision became *John Thomas and Lady Jane*, which also exists as a separate manuscript. It first appeared in an Italian translation in 1954, and was published in English in 1972. For the second version Lawrence began to insert many of the detailed descriptions of lovemaking that were to make the book so notorious: as Connie and Parkin make love for the first time in the cottage, Lawrence refers to 'the strange gallant phallus looking round in its odd bright godhead'; Connie puts 'her arms round [Parkin's] waist, and her swinging breasts touched the summit of the erect phallus in a sort of homage.' [52] The treatment of Clifford is also

---

[52] In early 1927 he was expending much of his energy painting, and told his friend Earl Brewster: 'I put a phallus in each one of my pictures somewhere. And I paint no picture that wont shock people's castrated social spirituality.' The penis was especially important as 'the river of the only God we can be sure about, the blood'. The evocation in these 1927 paintings is that of prelapsarian sexuality, the connection to what is basic and good and primaeval in life, and Lawrence's novel-writing and picture-making were to a large extent complementary activities.

different. In the first book, Clifford is Connie's intellectual equal. He satisfies her spiritually but not physically. Connie says in the first book: '[H]er two men were two halves. And she did not want to forfeit either half, to forego either man.' But in the second book Parkin has substantially won out. Clifford has become remote, childlike. The character of Parkin has also changed: among the more notable alterations is that he is given a strange new sexual past. He labours under a phobia reminiscent of that said to have bedevilled John Ruskin, in that during the first few weeks of his marriage he has been unable to have sex unless his wife's pubic hair is shaved off, because of an incident in his childhood when a 16-year old girl (later, in fact, his wife) exposed herself to him.

Lawrence finished *John Thomas and Lady Jane* in mid-February 1927, and let it lie fallow for most of the rest of the year. In November he began to draft for the third time, despite being very ill with tuberculosis, and finished it in six weeks. This third version was different again. New characters were introduced, such as the Irish playwright Michaelis, with whom Connie has an unsatisfactory affair ('Like so many modern men, [Michaelis] was finished almost before he had begun.') Parkin's name is now changed to Mellors, and he is a much more complex figure. He has received a good education, has served as an officer in the war, and is able to converse about ideas in a way that Parkin could not. He bridges the divide between the classes rather than remaining resolutely on one side. The novel ends with a long letter from Mellors to Connie in which Mellors articulates his philosophy of personal sexual togetherness, as against the pettiness of politics and money-making: 'I believe in the little flame between us. For me now, it's the only thing in the world. I've got no friends, not inward friends. Only you. [...] It's my Pentecost, the forked flame between me and you.' Mellors, in fact, seems very like Lawrence himself.

Now the only problem was what to call it. During the various drafts, Lawrence had experimented with a number of titles, among them *Tenderness*, *My Lady's Keeper* and *Lady Chatterley's Lover*, but none were satisfactory. Then inspiration came from someone who was rather disgusted by the whole business of Mellors and Connie. Lawrence had asked Juliette Huxley, the wife of Julian Huxley (the brother of Aldous) for her help in typing up the manuscript of the final version, but she couldn't get more than a few pages in without throwing it aside in horror. On March 9, 1928 Lawrence wrote to Aldous and Maria Huxley (his neighbours in Florence) about this final version and Juliette's reaction:

> Today I lunched with Orioli, and we took the MS of the novel to the printer: great moment. Juliette who read the MS and was very cross, morally so, suggested rather savagely that I should call it: 'John Thomas and Lady Jane'. Many a true word spoken in spite, so I promptly called it that. Remains to be seen if Secker and Knopf will stand it.

Why 'John Thomas and Lady Jane'? For this reason: these are the pet names that Mellors and Connie give to their respective private parts. The names appear in several places in the novel, most memorably in the famous scene in which Mellors decorates his godhead with flowers:

> He had brought columbines and campions, and new-mown hay, and oak-tufts and honeysuckle in small bud. He fastened fluffy young oak-sprays round her breasts, sticking in tufts of bluebells and campion: and in her navel he poised a pink campion flower, and in her maiden-hair were forget-me-nots and woodruff.
>
> 'That's you in all your glory!' he said. 'Lady Jane, at her wedding with John Thomas.'
>
> And he stuck flowers in the hair of his own body, and wound a bit of creeping-jenny round his penis, and stuck a single bell of a hyacinth in his navel. She watched him with amusement, his odd intentness. And she pushed a campion flower in his moustache, where it stuck, dangling under his nose.
>
> 'This is John Thomas marryin' Lady Jane,' he said.

A week later Lawrence had had second thoughts, partly persuaded by Aldous Huxley who said that *John Thomas and Lady Jane* would make it easy for customs officials who were looking for pornography. He changed it rather reluctantly back to *Lady Chatterley's Lover*. He wrote to Mabel Dodge Luhan on 13 March 1928, about the final version: 'Now I'm so busy with my novel. I want to call it "John Thomas and Lady Jane" ("John Thomas" is one of the names for the penis, as probably you know) but have to submit to put this as a sub-title, and continue with *Lady Chatterley's Lover* for the publisher's sake.'

After publishing privately in Italy, *Lady Chatterley's Lover* saw considerable critical and financial success as a piece of contraband goods, and Lawrence lived to enjoy this success before his death in March 1930. To defeat the customs men Lawrence also suggested some new titles. He wrote to Orioli, his Italian publisher, saying that he should arrange for some false dust-jackets to be printed to disguise the book. His suggestions for these false titles included *The Way of All Flesh* by Samuel Butler and *Joy Go With You* by Norman Kranzler.

All three Chatterley novels are still in print and are a unique record of the working-out of a major twentieth-century novel. It was, as Frieda Lawrence said, the book he was made for: 'All his life,' she said, 'he wanted to write *Lady Chatterley's Lover*.' And it seems clear that the final version should have been called not *Lady Chatterley's Lover* but *John Thomas and Lady Jane*, the title given many years later to the second draft. His last and most extraordinary book got a title a little less outrageous than it probably should have.

44

The Great American Novel (1973)
Philip Roth

ROTH'S *The Great American Novel* is a saga about baseball, narrated by an 87-year-old sports writer, Word Smith,
or 'Smitty' to his fans. Smitty's mission in life is to restore
the reputation of the (fictional) Patriot League, a baseball
league disbanded due to alleged Communist sympathies.
The novel's characters include Spit Baal, an ex-con known
as 'the Babe Ruth of the Big House', and Gil Gamesh, a
pitcher famous for once trying to kill the umpire. The whole
is set in the 1960s, the decade in which the Great America
that one might expect to be depicted in the Great American
Novel is falling apart in a bloodbath of assassinations, civil
unrest and wars. In the game of baseball, Roth dramatizes
the struggle between the promoters of the national myth,
with its tropes of military supremacy abroad and comfort
and prosperity at home, and the 'relentlessly insidious,
very nearly demonic reality' that confronts it.

It begins: 'Call me Smitty.'

Roth's novel is well titled, then, and about as ironic a title
as a title can be without imploding under its own weight

(for reasons I will explore more fully in a moment). But it is only one of a number of novels called *The Great American Novel*. Bailey Millard wrote one in 1897, William Carlos Williams produced another in 1923; others have been written by Clyde Brion Davis (1938), Eliot Stafford (2004) and Thomas A Brewster (2008). All have a concrete origin: all were responses to a challenge laid down in 1868 by John William De Forest, in an article in *The Nation* entitled 'The Great American Novel'.

De Forest was himself a novelist, and not an unsuccessful one. His books include *Witching Times* (1856), *Seacliff* (1859), *Miss Ravenel's Conversion* (1867), *Kate Beaumont* (1872) and *A Lover's Revolt* (1898). It was immediately after the publication of the best-known of these, *Miss Ravenel's Conversion* (showered with praise by reviewers as 'brilliant', 'extraordinary', 'one of the very best novels of which American literature can boast'), that he published an article in *The Nation* that was to have a permanent, and baleful, influence on American letters. This article was 'The Great American Novel' – a term he coined – on the state of American fiction in 1868, and it deserves quoting from at some length. In it De Forest said that a true depiction of American life had yet to be written:

> This task of painting the American soul within the
> framework of a novel has seldom been attempted, and
> has never been accomplished further than very partially
> – in the production of a few outlines. Washington Irving
> was too cautious to make the trial; he went back to
> fictions of Knickerbockers and Rip Van Winkles and Ich-

abod Cranes; these he did well, and we may thank him for not attempting more and failing in the attempt. With the same consciousness of incapacity Cooper shirked the experiment; he devoted himself to Indians, of whom he knew next to nothing, and to backwoodsmen and sailors, whom he idealized; or where he attempted civilized groups, he produced something less natural than the wax figures of Barnum's old museum. If all Americans were like the heroes and heroines of Cooper, Carlyle might well enough call us 'eighteen millions of bores'. As for a tableau of American society, as for anything resembling the tableaux of English society by Thackeray and Trollope, or the tableaux of French society by Balzac and George Sand, we had better not trouble ourselves with looking for it in Cooper. [...] Hawthorne, the greatest of American imaginations, staggered under the load of the American novel. In 'The Scarlet Letter', 'The House of the Seven Gables', and 'The Blithedale Romance' we have three delightful romances, full of acute spiritual analysis, of the light of other worlds, but also characterized by only a vague consciousness of this life, and by graspings that catch little but the subjective of humanity. Such personages that Hawthorne creates belong to the wide realm of art rather than to our nationality. They are as probably natives of the furthest mountains of Cathay or of the moon as of the United States of America. They are what Yankees might come to be who should shut themselves up for life to meditate in old manses. They have no sympathy with this eager and laborious people, which takes so many newspapers, builds so many railroads, does the most business on a given capital, wages the biggest war in proportion to its population, believes in the physically impossible and does some of it. [...] The profoundest reverence for this great man need prevent no one from saying that he has not written 'the Great American Novel'. The nearest approach to the desired phenomenon is 'Uncle Tom's Cabin'. There were very noticeable faults in that story; there was a very faulty plot; there was (if idealism be a fault) a black man painted whiter than the angels, and a girl such as girls are to be, perhaps, but are not yet; there was a little village twaddle. But there was also a national breadth to the picture, truthful outlining of character, natural speaking, and plenty of strong feeling. Though comeliness of form was lacking, the material of the work was in many respects admirable. [...] Then, stricken with timidity, the author shrank into her native shell of New England.

It is a remarkable essay, considering what was to come. Melville, Twain, James, Hemingway, Dos Passos, Fitzgerald, Faulkner, Wolfe – all were in the future in 1868 (Melville was strictly speaking in the present, but had not yet flitted across De Forest's radar). All of these writers must have been aware of De Forest's famous challenge, must have known of the phrase 'The Great American Novel' – often simply referred to simply as the GAN – and been aware of the implicit lack it described. All were goaded into action, at least in part, by the challenge of De Forest. The GAN, moreover, became a standard against which any American writer was judged. In 1872, four years after De Forest's essay, TS Perry wrote a denunciation of the whole idea of the GAN in the *North American Review*, slyly turning the phrase against its originator:

> We have often wondered that the people who raise the
> outcry for the 'Great American Novel' did not see that,
> so far from being of any assistance to our fellow-coun-
> tryman who is trying to win fame by writing fiction, they
> have rather stood in his way by setting up before him a
> false aim for his art, and by giving the critical reader a
> defective standard by which to judge his work. [...] Let us
> take, for example, Mr De Forest's novels. In his writings
> we find a great deal that is American, but not so much
> that goes to the making of a really great novel.

Later critics made similar points, complaining that America was far too diverse ever to be represented by one novel, and that any novel that was truly great would unavoidably see deeply into the human condition, as for example Tolstoy or Dickens had done, and thus not be a Great American Novel, but a Great World Novel. The term was doomed. Too specifically American and it could not be Great; too universal in its themes and it could not be usefully labelled American. Frank Norris in *The Responsibilities of the Novelist* said that '[T]he Great American Novel is not extinct like the Dodo, but mythical like the Hippogriff [...] the thing to be looked for is not the Great American Novelist, but the Great Novelist who shall also be an American.'

No-one cared. By the time Roth came to write *The Great American Novel*, the idea of the GAN had been festering in American literature for a hundred years. It had, for all that time, been encouraging American writers, chiefly male writers, to strive for Great Bloated Masterpieces (the idea of a female GAN seems inherently contradictory, which may indicate what was going wrong). Hemingway, Dos Passos, Fitzgerald, Faulkner, Wolfe...

But why was it that America felt it needed a Great Novel? Why was there not the same impetus towards a Great Australian Novel or a Great Moldovan Novel? Was it that, as a recently-formed nation, the USA still felt a sense of cultural inadequacy, as the country that had 'gone from barbarism to decadence without being civilized in between'? Or was there was guilt at being 'a nation founded on slavery and genocide,' as Kurt Vonnegut put it, the GAN being an attempt to foster national health and vitality, at least in the novelistic sphere?

When Philip Roth came to write his novel, the very notion of a GAN was patently a sign of some deep mental and spiritual distress. In one scene in his novel Roth envisions Hemingway inveighing against the GAN in language parodying Melville's Ahab:

'I feel deadly faint, bowed, and humped, as though
I were Adam, staggering beneath the piled centuries
since Paradise! God! God! God! – crack my heart – stave
my brain! – mockery! mockery! Close! Stand close to
me, Frederico; let me look into a human eye. The Great
American Novel. Why should Hemingway give chase to
the Great American Novel?'

'Good question, Papa. Keep it up and it's going to
drive you nuts.'

'What is it, Frederico, what nameless, inscrutable,
unearthly thing is it; what cozening, hidden lord and
master, and cruel, remorseless emperor commands me;
that against all natural lovings and longings, I so keep

pushing, and crowding, and jamming myself on all the time; recklessly making me ready to do what in my own proper, natural heart, I durst not so much as dare? Is Papa, Papa? Is it I, God, or who, that lifts this writing arm?' he asked, raising the pistol to his head.

'All right, Hem, that's enough now,' I said. 'You don't even sound like yourself. A book is a book, no more. Who would want to kill himself over a novel?'

Roth made no pretensions to writing the GAN in *The Great American Novel*, and when talking about his book in 1973 emphasized his lack of qualifications for the job, saying: 'I don't claim to know what America is "really like":'

> *Not* knowing, or no longer knowing for sure, is just what perplexes many of the people who live and work here and consider this country home. That, if I may say so, is why I invented that paranoid fantasist Word Smith – the narrator who calls himself Smitty – to be (purportedly) the author of *The Great American Novel*.

With that, Roth's *Great American Novel* might have been the end of the GAN, save for the fact that the GAN is seemingly hardwired into the American literary consciousness. Novels continue to be published with pretensions to the crown, some of them even under the title *The Great American Novel*, as if by so titling their books authors will ironize themselves into literary immensity.

The day when all can agree that the GAN is dead will be a healthy day for American literature, but it seems a long way off.

45

The Amityville Horror: A True Story (1977)
Jay Anson

ON December 18, 1975, George and Kathy Lutz buy an
eerie, pumpkin-eye-windowed Dutch Colonial Barn at 112
Ocean Avenue, Amityville, New York, and move in with
their three children. They are not a whit disconcerted that
the house has recently been the scene of a notorious murder, in which a young man named Ronnie DeFeo has shot
his parents and four siblings. They are simply glad to get
the house at a bargain price. But shortly after they take up
residence, odd things begin to happen. The ceilings and
floors start to ooze green slime. Cloven hoofprints appear
in the snow outside. The telephone service becomes unre-
liable; chilling cold is observed; a ceramic lion is moved
(possibly teleported); there is a nauseating stench in the
basement; there are recurrent plagues of flies; the inside
of a toilet bowl turns black; a crucifix in Kathy's closet is
inverted; and the family dog starts behaving strangely,
going to sleep at odd times. They call in a priest but it is to
no avail. After twenty-eight days, the Lutzes reach break-
ing point and leave. The end.

The plot of *The Amityville Horror* is not very original, deriving ultimately from Poe ('The Fall of the House of Usher') and from the haunted house formula in American fiction in general. Motifs to do with an ancient curse – the Amityville house has formerly been inhabited by one 'Jack Catchum or Ketcham [...] forced out of Salem, Massachusetts, for practising witchcraft' – are straight out of Hawthorne (*The House of the Seven Gables*). It ends with the familiar and satisfying notion that the crimes of the past have consequences, and that there is a real supernatural world, one that gives the lie to our present limited scientific worldview.

Nor was the title very original. It came, in fact, from HP Lovecraft. In 1928 Lovecraft had written the short story 'The Dunwich Horror' (see chapter 21), in which a young man, in an attempt to get at the accursed *Necronomicon*, is killed by a police dog; later in the story, his house is revealed to be the hiding-place for an gargantuan transdimensional Thing that ravages the countryside, killing cattle. 'The Dunwich Horror' was also set in New England and was made into a movie in 1970, only five years before the supposed events of *The Amityville Horror*. George Lutz, in fact, confirmed that this was the source of the title: Jay Anson, the author of the book, had 'pulled it from a work done by someone years earlier called "The Dunwich Horror".'

So why, if *The Amityville Horror* was so derivative, was it so successful? Sales of the book reached the tens of millions and it was made into no less than nine movies. Here the second element of the title comes in: it was *The Amityville Horror: A True Story*. This claim is quite unusual in the haunted house formula. George and Kathy Lutz really existed; they really *did* buy the house on Ocean Avenue, really *did* leave a month later, and really *did* go on chat shows to talk about it. 'More hideously frightening than *The Exorcist* because it actually happened!' screamed the paperback front cover. Throughout the book – written up by Jay Anson from their tape-recorded testimony – there is an emphasis on the complete factuality of the story. The book begins with the claim that 'all facts and events, as far as we have been able to verify them, are strictly accurate.' There is a Preface, Prologue and Afterword to the main text, as appropriate to any document of dry and dogged insistence on complete objectivity. The Afterword reads: 'George Lee and Kathleen Lutz undertook the exhaustive and frequently painful task of reconstructing their twenty-eight days in the house in Amityville on a tape recorder, refreshing each other's memories so that the final oral 'diary' would be as complete as possible [...] I should point out, too, that when the Lutzes fled their home in early 1976, they had not thought of putting their experiences into book form.'

Unfortunately, this last point was later disputed. It just so happened that the Lutzes were friends with William Weber, the former defence lawyer of Ronnie DeFeo, the murderer at the house. And in 1979 Weber claimed that the whole *Amityville* story was pure invention. 'We created this horror story over many bottles of wine that George Lutz was drinking,' he said in an interview. 'We were creating something the public wanted to hear about.' He said that the Lutzes couldn't afford the mortgage, and that this was their real motive for leaving the house. His own motive was to use the 'demonic possession' angle to get a new trial for his client. Then the friends fell out: Weber, seeing the immense profits the Lutzes were making over a story that they had cooked up jointly, wanted a piece of the action. The floodgates opened and hellish legal writs came pouring out. The Lutzes sued Weber and Weber the Lutzes; the new residents of 112 Ocean Avenue sued the Lutzes for compensation because their property was overrun by thrill-seeking horror fans; other litigants included *Good Housekeeping* magazine and the Hearst Corporation. Judge Jack B Weinstein in the Weber vs Lutz case concluded in 1979: 'The evidence shows fairly clearly that the Lutzes during this entire period were considering and acting with the thought of having a book published.'

Perhaps Weber and the Lutzes were students of Freud. In 'The Uncanny', an essay of 1919, Freud noted that a particular vein of feeling that he termed *unheimlich* – translated as 'uncanny' – is created when an artist invokes the ordinary world of mundane experience and then shows it to be utterly unfamiliar, as when a doll's eyes suddenly flicker into life. The Amityville story with its claim of veracity did much the same thing. As Freud put it:

> The souls in Dante's *Inferno* or the ghostly apparitions
> in Shakespeare's *Hamlet*, *Macbeth*, or *Julius Caesar* may
> be dark and terrifying, but at bottom they are no more
> uncanny than, say, the serene Gods of Homer. [...] Not

so, however, if the writer has to all appearances taken up his stance on the ground of common reality. By doing so he adopts all the conditions that apply to the emergence of a sense of the uncanny in normal experience; whatever has an uncanny effect in real life has the same in literature. But the writer can intensify and multiply this effect far beyond what is feasible in normal experience; in his stories he can make things happen that one would never, or only rarely, experience in real life. In a sense, then, he betrays us to a superstition we thought we had 'surmounted'; he tricks us by promising us everyday reality and then going beyond it.

46

Blade Runner (a movie) (1979)
William S Burroughs

THE 1982 film *Blade Runner* by Ridley Scott deals with a bounty hunter, played by Harrison Ford, who is tasked to 'retire' fugitive androids. There are no blades particularly visible in it; and although there is plenty of running, it is unclear who might be doing the running in the title.

It's necessary to take two steps back, and one step to the side, to understand.

In 1974, the US sci-fi writer Alan E Nourse published a book called *The Bladerunner*. The back cover blurb explained:

> Billy Gimp was a bladerunner... one of the shadowy procurers of illegal medical supplies for the rapidly expanding, nightmare world of the medical black market. Doc was a skilled surgeon at a government-operated hospital by day... and an underground physician by night, providing health care for the multitudes who could not – or would not qualify for legal medical assistance.

The problem is one familiar to Americans in the age of Obama: a divisive healthcare system in which money determines who thrives and who dies. Except that in this case, medical care for the poor has actually become illegal. 'Bladerunners' – or carriers of scalpels for illicit operations – are necessary to keep the poor alive.

The book was a modest success, and William S Burroughs, the notorious author of *Junkie* and *Naked Lunch*, was commissioned to write a story treatment – aptly enough, since *The Bladerunner* had all the ingredients of a Burroughs dystopia, being preoccupied with drugs, shady doctors and urban breakdown. In 1979 Burroughs produced the novella *Blade Runner (a movie)*, dedicated to Nourse, 'upon whose book, *The Blade Runner*, characters and situations in this book are based'. Burroughs' book was not a movie, nor a screenplay for a movie in any conventional sense; instead it was a loose collection of scenes and ideas that *might* have been made into a movie (though, as things turned out, they never were). *Blade Runner (a movie)* is a much more accomplished and entertaining read than *The Bladerunner*: Burroughs does not stint himself on such matters as the sale of unpolluted boy-sperm or the correct deployment of cross-bows loaded with sodium cyanide. He also develops the general plot:

> By 1980, pressure had been growing to put through a National Health Act. This was blocked by the medical lobby, doctors protesting that such an Act would mean the virtual end of private practice, and that the overall quality of medical services would decline. The strain

on an already precarious economy was also cited. Drug
companies, fearing that price regulation would slash
profits, spent millions to lobby against the proposed
bill and ran full-page ads in all the leading newspapers.
And above all, the health insurance companies screamed
that the Act was unnecessary and could only lead to
increased taxes for inferior service.

[...]

The Health Act soon poses more problems than it solves.
Drugs to halt the ageing process have brought life expec-
tancy up to 125 years, thus aggravating the population
problem. On the other hand, illnesses which have seemingly been eliminated suddenly erupt in epidemic form,
like the deadly adult diphtheria which broke out in the
later 1980s. The population, drenched with increasingly
effective antibiotics, had lost all natural resistance and
become as vulnerable to these infections as the Indians
and South Sea Islanders on their first contact with the
whites.

A Health Amendment Act is brought in to try to solve the
problem by restricting access to medical care.

The unfit were to be denied medical service of any kind
unless they agreed to sterilization, 'Unfitness' to be
determined by a board of doctors and vaguely defined
as 'suffering from any hereditary illness, condition or
tendency deemed to be biologically undesirable'. Like
being a nigger...or a wog... or a queer... or a dope
fiend... or a psychopath... HAA HAA HAA.

The blade runners become necessary to supply the new demand, finding their way across the shattered city by means of flooded subway tunnels.

But this still has no obvious relation to the Ridley Scott film, which does not explore health care, and contains no illicit doctors or scalpel-couriers.

In the early 1980s Ridley Scott was the highly successful director of *Alien* (1979). Casting around for an idea for his next project, he happened upon Philip K Dick's 1968 novel *Do Androids Dream of Electric Sheep?* and acquired the rights. *Do Androids Dream of Electric Sheep?* was the real basis of the film *Blade Runner*. Dick's book is a meditation on the nature of human identity. In the aftermath of a nuclear war the inhabitants of Earth are encouraged to leave their poisoned planet and settle on off-world colonies: each colonist is given an android to accompany him (some are even supplied with an entire family next door – or 'famnexdo' – to make them feel comfortable). But the androids are so sophisticated that they themselves become discontented, and rebel against their masters. Like spawning salmon, they keep trying to make it back to the place of their birth. It is Rick Deckard's job to hunt and kill them.

The novel was developed into a screenplay by writers Hampton Fancher and David Peoples, who abandoned or stripped out much of the detail of the book, but kept the main plot. Ridley Scott however worried about the corniness of the terms 'bounty hunter' and 'android' and wondered whether substitutions could be invented. It was at this point that Fancher came across Burroughs' book, and realized that the evocative phrase 'blade runner' could be elliptically applied to the activities of Rick Deckard. The rights to the title and the phrase 'blade runner' were consequently bought from Burroughs and Nourse. 'Replicant', the replacement for 'android', was David Peoples' contribution: the term was suggested by his daughter, a microbiologist, who thought that something to do with 'replication' might offer an attractive neologism.

Thus was *Blade Runner*, the movie, created, with its denatured world of giant advertising and immense ziggurats, vampish forties dames and private dicks, punks and monks, all in a setting combining Tokyo and Gotham City; it became one of the most innovative sci-fi films ever made. One very welcome side-effect was that it gave a cardiac jolt to the ailing reputation of Philip K Dick, whose work had been out of print for some years. Dick was asked to write the novelization of the film, but instead opted to re-issue his own *Do Androids Dream of Electric Sheep?* – though it appeared in bookshops under the title *Blade Runner*. Several of his other works were also later reprinted, notably the short story 'We Can Remember It For You Wholesale', which was made into the movie *Total Recall*. Unfortunately Dick died in 1982 without having seen *Blade Runner*.

The story illustrates one rather astonishing thing: that a good title, if good enough, and even if only two words, can stand alone, without any link at all to the actual contents of the new work it announces.

47

Dogg's Hamlet, Cahoot's Macbeth (1979)
Tom Stoppard

DOGG'S *Hamlet* and *Cahoot's Macbeth* are two short
plays written to be performed together. *Dogg's Hamlet* is a play that has fun with Wittgenstein. Stoppard
explained in his introduction to the printed edition
that at the time of its composition he had been reading
Wittgenstein's *Philosophical Investigations,* and had been
struck by a passage in which the philosopher invited his
readers to imagine two men building a wall. The first
man shouts out 'Plank!' and is thrown a plank. He then
shouts out 'Block!' and is thrown a block. He shouts
'Cube!' and is thrown a cube. An observer who does not
speak their language might assume that the words refer
to shapes and sizes of building materials, but an equally
likely scenario is that the first man is just saying 'Ready!'
'OK!' or 'Next!', indicating his desire to be thrown something, and the second man is so familiar with the task of
building the wall that he always throws him the right
piece. Stoppard went on:

In such a case, the observer would have made a false assumption, but the fact that he on the one hand and the builders on the other are using two different languages need not be apparent to either party. Moreover, it would also be possible that the two builders do not share a language either; if life for them consisted only of building platforms in this manner there would be no reason for them to discover that each was using a language unknown to the other. This happy state of affairs would of course continue only as long as, through sheer coincidence, each man's utterance made sense (even if not the same sense) to the other. The appeal to me consisted in the possibility of writing a play which had to teach the audience the language the play was written in. The present text is a modest attempt to do this: I think one might have gone much further.

The play begins with this very scenario, that of two men building a wall and calling out to one another, though they are soon interrupted by some schoolboys who are rehearsing a production of *Hamlet*. However, the schoolboys speak only a language called Dogg (also the name of one of the characters, a schoolmaster). The English of Shakespeare is therefore to them a foreign tongue. What makes matters slightly confusing (and amusing) is that Dogg consists of English words, sometimes with meanings opposite to the ones we are familiar with. In the printed edition of the play Stoppard supplied a translation, but in performance the audience were expected to work it out for themselves:

ABEL: (*Respectfully, to DOGG.*) Cretinous, git? [What time is it, sir?]

DOGG: (*Turning round.*) Eh?

ABEL: Cretinous pig-faced, git? [Have you got the time please, sir?]

(*DOGG takes a watch out of his waistcoat pocket and examines it.*)

DOGG: Trog poxy [Half-past three.]

ABEL: Cube, git. [Thank you, sir.]

The schoolboys, after giving the audience a crash-course in Dogg, then launch into a version of *Hamlet* in English, which, though severely edited, is played relatively straight. *Dogg's Hamlet* consists of two halves, therefore, which are more or less unrelated. The reason for this lies in the history of the play, clues to which are buried in the title.

The story begins with Ed Berman, a Harvard-trained archaeologist who founded a theatre group called Inter-Action in London in the late 1960s. Berman staged an early play of Stoppard's, *After Magritte*, in 1970, at the Green Banana restaurant in Soho, and then, in 1971, after Inter-Action had moved to the Almost Free Theatre on Rupert Street (so called because the public were invited to suggest a contribution as the price of admittance), directed another play by Stoppard called *Dogg's Our Pet*, the original version of *Dogg's Hamlet*. *Dogg's Our Pet* featured the Wittgensteinian hi-jinks already mentioned, but didn't include the *Hamlet*. The origin of the title *Dogg's Our Pet* is convoluted in the extreme. Berman ran a children's theatre group called Dogg's Troupe, so called because it was led by one Professor RL Dogg (Berman himself). The name RL Dogg was designed to appear in card catalogues as 'Dogg, RL', which, when said aloud, is 'doggerel'. Stoppard commented that 'anyone who could wait that long for a pun to explode deserved better,' and wrote *Dogg's Our Pet* as Berman's reward: *Dogg's Our Pet* is an anagram of 'Dogg's Troupe'. At around the same time, Stoppard was working on a 15-minute version of *Hamlet* to be staged on Berman's Fun Art Bus – a converted double-decker bus with, in Berman's words, 'the smallest proscenium arch in the world installed on the upper deck'. This 15-minute *Hamlet* finally merged with *Dogg's Our Pet* – the play that has fun with Wittgenstein – in 1979, to make *Dogg's Hamlet*.

Berman by this time had founded the British American Repertory Company (whose acronym, as readers will see, is the most appropriate for an ensemble led by a Dogg) and asked Stoppard if he would write a short play for it. This became *Cahoot's Macbeth*. This is another title rich in hidden meaning.

Stoppard was born into a Jewish family in Czechoslovakia in 1937. His parents fled the country just before the outbreak of the Second World War, finally settling in England. 'Stoppard' was the name of his mother's second husband, his father having been killed in the war, and Tom (originally Tomáš) was brought up speaking English. Only in the 1970s did he begin to explore fully his Czech identity. This was of course the era of Soviet occupation and the post-Dub□ek crackdown, a time when

Czechoslovakia was, as Stoppard put it, 'an upside-down country where you can find boilers stoked by economists, streets swept by men reading Henry James in English'. His plays became more concerned with political themes, and he began to have contacts with playwrights including Václav Havel, whose plays he adapted into English. His political involvement extended to speaking in Trafalgar Square against 'psychiatric abuse' in Czechoslovakia – the practice of imprisoning political dissidents in mental hospitals – and he supported Charter 77, the document signed by Czech intellectuals demanding greater political freedoms. Stoppard travelled to Prague in June 1977 to meet Havel, who had recently been released from prison, and it was from this visit that *Cahoot's Macbeth* emerged. 'Cahoot', which to an English audience suggests 'cahoots', in the conspiracy sense, was in fact named after a Czecho-slovakian playwright, Pavel Kohout, who Stoppard met briefly on this trip in 1977. Theatre in Czechoslovakia had been heavily restricted, and Kohout, in response, had devised a 'reduced' Macbeth that could be performed out of a suitcase in the living-room of a Prague flat. This was LRT, or Living-Room Theatre. Kohout wrote to Stoppard in June 1978:

> What is LRT? A call-group. Everybody, who wants to
> have Macbeth at home with two great and forbidden
> Czech actors, Pavel Landovský and Vlasta Chramostová,
> can invite his friends and call us. Five people will come
> with one suitcase.

Kohout's LRT presented a seventy-five-minute version of *Macbeth*, about half the normal run-time, and was thus strikingly similar in concept to the reduced Shakespeare of the 15-minute *Hamlet*. Stoppard decided to write a tribute to Kohout: *Cahoot's Macbeth*. The plot concerns a group of players performing the living-room version of *Macbeth*, who are interrupted by an inspector from the secret police:

> INSPECTOR: [...] Well, I'll tell you what. I don't want to spend all day taking statements. It's frankly not worth the candle for three years' maximum and I know you've been having a run of bad luck all round – jobs lost, children failing exams, letters undelivered, driving licenses withdrawn, passports indefinitely postponed – and nothing on paper. It's as if the system had a mind of its own; so why don't you give it a chance, and I'll give you one. I'm really glad I caught you before you closed.

At the play's end one of the characters from *Dogg's Hamlet* turns up to make a delivery of blocks and cubes à la Wittgenstein, and begins speaking incomprehensibly in Dogg. The players are at first baffled, but after a while they cotton on: everyone begins speaking in Dogg, except the secret policeman, who is unable to adapt quickly enough to the mercurial nature of the moment, and suspects (rightly) that this is one more attempt at subversion. The Dogg-language and the Shakespeare-language are thus neatly tied together as paired modes of resistance, and the two plays, *Dogg's Hamlet* and *Cahoot's Macbeth*, suddenly gel.

The two plays are among Stoppard's most exciting and complex productions, combining as they do linguistic exploration, political satire, physical farce and absurdist humour. And the stories behind both plays are enfolded, almost archaeologically, in the titles.

48

The Name of the Rose (1980)
Umberto Eco

THE Name of the Rose is the most unlikely of all bestsellers.
Suffused with postmodern literary theory, it spends much
of its time discussing medieval theological controversies
in untranslated Latin. Perhaps it is the series of gruesome
murders (drowning in pigs' blood, burning alive, death
by poisoned book, etc.) that propelled it to the top of the
charts. Without the murders, *The Name of the Rose* would
surely never have sold 10 million copies, been translated
into 30 languages, and made into a film starring Sean Connery and Christian Slater.

The story is set in a Benedictine abbey, where a Fran-
ciscan friar, William of Baskerville (one of many nods to
Conan Doyle), and his assistant, Adso of Melk, have been
summoned to mediate in a religious dispute. No sooner
do they arrive than the homicides begin. The illuminator
Adelmo of Otranto falls – or is pushed – to his death. Then
another monk is found face down in a jar of pigs' blood
– though he may have been placed there to make it look
as if he has drowned. William investigates, his opponent

being Jorge of Burgos, a blind librarian, a playful invocation of the blind novelist Jorge Luis Borges. After five more
bizarre deaths the truth about the abbey and its mysterious
library is revealed.

What has this got to do with roses? Eco wrote in an essay,
'The Author and his Interpreters':

> An author who has entitled his book *The Name of the Rose*
> must be ready to face manifold interpretations of his
> title. As an empirical author I wrote that I chose that title
> just in order to set the reader free: 'the rose is a figure
> so rich in meanings that by now it hasn't any meaning:
> Dante's mystic rose, and go lovely rose, the War of the
> Roses, rose thou art sick, too many rings around Rosie, a
> rose by any other name, a rose is a rose is a rose is a rose,
> the Rosicrucians.'

Elsewhere, in his 'Postscript to the Name of the Rose' (published in the 1984 Harcourt translation of the novel), he
goes further:

> The title rightly disoriented the reader, who was unable
> to choose just one interpretation [...] A title must muddle
> the reader's ideas, not regiment them.

So the title was deliberately obscure. Why be so cruel to the
reader? One explanation might be found in the text itself.
The novel's subject is, partly, signs – and signs as clues –
which have various ecclesiastical, theological, political and
social meanings. Signs may point to the truth – as in the
opening chapter, where William deduces from a horse's

hoofprints that the Abbot's mount has bolted – but may also mislead, so that the unwary are led into error. And this is precisely what does happen to William, who, although he uncovers the secrets behind the murders, does so for completely the wrong reasons. As he tells Adso at the book's conclusion:

> I arrived at Jorge through an apocalyptic pattern that seemed to underlie all the crimes, and yet it was acciden-tal. I arrived at Jorge seeking one criminal for all the crimes and we discovered that each crime was commit-ted by a different person, or by no one. I arrived at Jorge pursuing the plan of a perverse and rational mind, and there was no plan [...] Where is all my wisdom, then?

The rose is a signifier of such multivalency that it will inevitably deceive and frustrate the literal-minded. A good choice, then, for a book about the multivalency of signs. Except that this is not quite the final word on *The Name of the Rose*.

In fact the last line of this 500-page novel does contain a reference to a rose, in a Latin hexameter by Bernard of Cluny: *Stat rosa pristina nomine, nomina nuda tenemus.* This can be translated as: 'The rose of yore exists in name alone; mere names we hold.' Again we are in the field of semiology, with a medieval twist: Bernard is saying that all things, including roses, leave only names behind them when they die, and that everything else disappears into the void. Even the greatest of empires crumble to dust, leav-ing only words, terms, behind them, which are their only continuing reality (if one discounts the speculations of the nominalists, who would argue that names have an ideal, universal existence, as in Plato's realm of forms).

In a sense, then, *The Name of the Rose* is that most respectable of all things, a quotation-title. Except that there is a further complication. The Latin hexameter is interesting because 'rose' here seems to have been a misreading by Eco of the original text. Other Bernard of Cluny texts refer to 'Rome' ('*Roma*' as opposed to '*rosa*', a one-letter slip). Eco realized this only later, and admitted the mix-up in a lecture at The Italian Academy for Advanced Studies in America:

> Moreover someone has discovered that some early manuscripts of *De contempu mundi* of Bernard de Cluny, from which I borrowed the hexameter 'stat rosa pristina nomine, nomina nuda tenemus,' read 'stat Roma pristina nomine' – which after all is more coherent with the rest of the poem, which speaks of the lost Babylonia. Thus the title of my novel, had I come across another version of Cluny's poem, could have been *The Name of Rome* (thus acquiring fascist overtones).'

The case for 'the name of Rome' as against 'the name of the rose' is fortified if one considers the lines immediately preceding the quotation, which speak of Rome and Roman doings:

> Where now are Marius and Fabricius who knew not gold?
> Where the noble death and memorable course of Paulus?

> Where now the divine Philippics, and the heavenly
> voice of Cicero?
> Where Cato's peacefulness to his countrymen and
> wrath against the rebellious foe?
> Where now is Regulus? Or Romulus? Or Remus?
> The Rome of yore exists in name alone; mere names
> we hold.

It seems almost certain, then, that the title *The Name of the Rose*, chosen because it was meaningless, was not merely meaningless, but an accident, making it doubly meaningless: a meaningless accident.

Does it matter? Perhaps not, if *The Name of the Rose* is a good read. Or perhaps it does, and the moral to be extracted from the book is that it is not always wise to heed semioticians.

49

Difficulties with Girls (1988)
Kingsley Amis

DIFFICULTIES *with Girls* is a sequel to Amis's earlier novel *Take a Girl Like You* (1960). It has the same couple at its centre, Patrick and Jenny Standish (formerly Jenny Bunn). In the sequel they are still married, though childless, and seven years older (real time has thus advanced four times as fast as novel time). Patrick has aged but not seen the error of his ways: he is still is a boozing philanderer, unable to resist any and every comer, including the next-door neighbour, Wendy Porter-King (a woman he despises to the point of wishing to knock her teeth out). In fact Patrick has the standard Amis 'difficulties with girls', largely arising from the fact that, as he sees it, females can't think logically, are selfish egomaniacs, weep at a moment's notice, and so on. Or as Amis put it in an unpublished poem he was writing at about the same time:

> Women and queers and children
> Cry when things go wrong:

> Not fair! – why me? – can't take it!
> [So] drones/sounds their dismal [eternal] song.

Jenny is a stay-at-home wife, still highly attractive and faithful, occupying herself with decorating their flat and pressing Patrick's trousers. She continues to struggle with her husband's imperfections and infidelities, which she knows all about, though she has given up confronting him over them. (Reviews made conspicuous mention of the impossible perfection of Jenny: the *New York Review of Books* called her 'the male chauvinist pig's dream girl, forever making cups of milky coffee for her circle of male admirers, tormenters and lame ducks.') The other characters in the novel comprise Tim Valentine, a sexually confused friend who thinks he might be gay, and a *bona fide* 'out' gay couple, Eric Davidson and Stevie Bairstow (names that are surely suspiciously close, when transposed, to Eric Bristow and Steve Davis, two of the most prominent pub sportsmen of the 1980s). The novel, then, contains quite a large dose of thematic homosexuality, unusual in an Amis novel. It reflects, perhaps, how the book was originally conceived. For in the earliest version of *Difficulties with Girls*, the hero had 'difficulties' of a completely different order. He was homosexual. Amis in fact spent a year creating a gay *Lucky Jim*.

The original *Difficulties with Girls* was begun in October 1980, and featured a narrator in the person of one Robert, a university student. Robert is gay, and is given the standard equipment for a gay man as Amis conceives it:

he has a love of gardening and home furnishings, and is content to be a babysitter and chauffeur for the novel's two other main characters, Ann and Adrian Marriot. The cast is completed by Adrian's brother Reggie and his wife Paula (with whom Adrian is having an affair), and an American student, Tom Vaccaro, who, like Tim Valentine in the completed novel, is unsure of his sexuality and has been seeing a psychiatrist (Tom Valentine and Tim Vaccarro have the same initials). But Amis, though he struggled with the novel, finally gave up on it, and nine months after first putting pen to paper, abandoned it. It now exists only in manuscript form in the Huntington Library, California. Amis said in an interview in 1984: 'Usually my novels obey the course that I set them. I may change my mind a bit as I go, but not much. This time the whole plan got entirely out of hand and I wasn't going to finish the thing.' Only the title survived – originally, of course, referring slyly to a major 'difficulty' with girls, that of being attracted instead to men – to be transferred to a totally new book.[53]

So why did Kingsley Amis ditch the 'gay hero' idea? It would have constituted an interesting departure for a late Amis novel. But it seems that it was not inspiration or talent that failed him, but nerve. According to his son Martin, he was worried that his cronies at the Garrick Club would think *he* was gay. Martin Amis wrote:

---

53 As it happens, this is not a very uncommon strategy in titling. *Seven Pillars of Wisdom* by TE Lawrence was originally the title of a different book about seven middle-eastern cities, but was transferred to his epic about battling in sand. *Never Let Me Go* by Kazuo Ishiguro is another case in point. It was originally the title of an earlier, uncompleted work about struggling song-writers, and later grafted on to his novel about cloning.

> I couldn't believe it. That was supposed to be the *point*
> of Kingsley Amis: he didn't care what people thought
> about him. 'Let me get this straight,' I said, gathering my
> argument. 'You're giving up a year's work because a few
> old wrecks at the Garrick, who probably think you're
> also a Northerner [*Lucky Jim*] and a Taff [*That Uncertain
> Feeling*], may suspect, wrongly, and semi-literately, and
> against the evidence of all the other books, that you're
> queer.' '...*Yeah THAT'S right*,' he answered.

This is confirmed by a letter from Kingsley Amis to Philip
Larkin of December 17, 1982:

> I did 130pp v. slowly and unenjoyably, then shelved it.
> Thing was, it was supposed to be going to be an account
> of a couple of marriages, i.e. the hetero world, seen by a
> 1st-person queer – for distancing, unexpectedness etc.,
> plus him being talked in front of and confided in in a
> way not open to a hetero. But it turned out, as you'd
> expect from a queer, to be all about him and being queer,
> which doesn't sort of appeal to me enough. And of
> course since only about 17 people in the country know
> what a novel is, the rest will think I must be one of the
> boys myself.

The completed *Difficulties with Girls* is not, in most critics' estimations, a major Amis novel, and it is tempting
to think that if Amis had stuck with his original concep-
tion he might have achieved something remarkable. But
Amis's biographer Zachary Leader calls the treatment of
gay life in the Huntington manuscript 'thinly textured'

and the character of Tom Vaccarro 'tediously obtuse and implausible'; and neither does Martin Amis put the quality of it very high, saying: 'It isn't without interest or insight, but it has a stalled feel.' Ultimately Kingsley Amis, not unusually for a man of his generation, had only limited sympathy for or understanding of gay men, and this seems to have seriously compromised the original draft. The main character would only talk in the way 'you'd expect from a queer' – and who would want to read that?

50

Generation X: Tales for an Accelerated Culture
(1991)
Douglas Coupland

GENERATION X is about three friends, Claire, Andy,
and Dag, who live together in Palm Springs, California,
some time in the late 1980s. They are in their twenties,
well-educated, intelligent, middle-class, the sons and
daughters of the 'baby-boom generation' of the immediate post-war period (read 'hippies'). They are surrounded
by all by the good things that a highly-developed con-
sumer society can provide, yet are strangely enfeebled,
regarding the world with a jaundiced eye; they work in
'McJobs' rather than pursuing real careers, and do very
little except fritter away their time by the swimming-
pool, telling each other stories.

Such was the novel, and at first it was not a very great
success. But then a film-maker called Richard Linklater
released a movie called *Slacker*, which became a low-
budget hit. It too featured alienated twenty-somethings
devoid of any purpose in life, wandering from one scene
to another in defiance of any conventional plot. At the

same time the music known as 'grunge' took off, particularly the song 'Smells Like Teen Spirit' by Nirvana. Kurt Cobain and Courtney Love, Janeane Garofalo and Eddie Vedder became household names, and Seattle, chain-store coffee, the first home computers and MTV somehow all got mixed up in it: suddenly everyone seemed aware that a new generation of young people had reached maturity (though maturity was probably the wrong word). These were young people who had been born sometime after 1961 and before 1979 – or between 1963 and 1975, 1965 and 1981, or just sometime in the 60s or 70s, according to taste – young people who couldn't remember the Vietnam War, the assassination of Kennedy or the speeches of Martin Luther King. And Douglas Coupland had noticed them first, and had given this Starbucks-bothering, ripped-jeans-wearing, pierced and irony-saturated generation a name: 'Generation X'. By the end of 1991 Coupland's book was a best-seller. What came next was almost uniquely distasteful. Coupland said in a 1995 interview for the men's magazine *Details*:

> Then the marketing began. Urban Outfitters. Those Bud ads where people rehash 60s TV sitcoms. Flavapalooza. Irony, which most young people use in order to make ludicrous situations palatable, was for the first time used as a selling tool. This demographic pornography was probably what young people resented most about the whole X explosion. I mean, sure, other fringe movements of the past - the 20s expats in Paris, the 50s Beats, 60s Hippies, 70s Punks - all got marketed in the end, but

X got hypermarketed right from the start, which was harsh.

Around this time my phone started ringing with corporations offering from $10,000 and up to talk on the subject of How to Sell to Generation X. I said no. [...] In late 1991, after both political parties had called to purchase advice on X, I basically withdrew from the whole tinny discourse.

In the same interview he also explained the origin of the title:

The book's title came not from Billy Idol's band, as many supposed, but from the final chapter of a funny sociological book on American class structure titled *Class*, by Paul Fussell. In his final chapter, Fussell named an 'X' category of people who wanted to hop off the merry-go-round of status, money, and social climbing that so often frames modern existence. The citizens of X had much in common with my own socially disengaged characters; hence the title. The book's title also allowed Claire, Andy, and Dag to remain enigmatic individuals while at the same time making them feel a part of the larger whole.

The origin of the title was eminently respectable, then: it came from an obscure work of sociology, the sort of text that one of Coupland's heroes might have read at college. But was this believable? Fussell's term was 'Class X', not 'Generation X'; and 'Generation X', as a phrase, already had wide currency. It had already been the title of a book, in fact: Jane Deverson and Charles Hamblett's

1964 study *Generation X: Today's Generation Talking About Itself.*

The story behind this earlier *Generation X* is as follows. In 1963 Jane Deverson had been commissioned by *Woman's Own* magazine to give an account of the opinions of the teenagers of the mid-1960s, and after conducting numerous interviews, had reached the shocking conclusion that the young people of the time had sex before marriage, didn't believe in God, disliked the Queen and didn't respect parents. *Woman's Own* refused to publish the data, but Deverson was convinced it was important, and teamed up with another journalist, Charles Hamblett, to produce a book. It was Hamblett who gave the young people the name 'Generation X', probably influenced partly by the name of the civil rights leader Malcolm X – who had changed his surname from 'Little' to 'X' as a rejection of the norms of white American society – and possibly also by the 'Brand X' of TV advertising. Their book sold well, and among the people who bought it was the mother of Billy Idol, the punk rocker. In 1976 Billy saw the book lying around the house and decided that its title was a good name for a band. Generation X, the band, became highly successful, particularly in the USA, with hits including 'Your Generation'. In *Vista* magazine in 1989 (still two years before the publication of the novel), when explaining the origin of the phrase, Coupland overstepped both Fussell and Deverson and went straight for Idol:

> Don, like so many people I know in their twenties, can do anything he wants, but instead he is doing nothing. Or, rather, he is doing many things, but there is no seeming

pattern and he has no long-range plan in mind. [...] Los
Angeles sociologist Susan Littwin calls people like Don
members of The Postponed Generation, in her 1986 book
of the same title. British punk rock star Billy Idol calls
them Generation X.

So when Coupland first wrote of Generation X he had his
phrase ready-made, pre-digested, a cliché before its time, a
rogue signifier loaded with the freight of several previous
decades. It already indicated a generation disenfranchised,
alienated and cool – though, rather ironically, the original
Generation X were the very post-war baby-boomers that
the 'slacker' generation of Coupland's novel were rebel-
ling against.

Sources and further reading

Items are presented in order of the chapter they refer to. Primary texts are given at the beginning of each paragraph.

Dante Alighieri: *The Divine Comedy* (c.1315; trans. Dorothy L Sayers, Penguin Classics, 1949)

Caesar, Michael, ed.: *Dante: The Critical Heritage* (Routledge, 1989)

Terpening, Ronnie H: *Lodovico Dolce, Renaissance Man of Letters* (University of Toronto Press, 1997)

White, Richard Grant, ed.: *The Works of William Shakespeare* (Little, Brown, 1865)

Caso, Adolph, ed.: *Romeo and Juliet: Original Text of Masuccio Salernitano, Luigi Da Porto, Matteo Bandello, William Shakespeare* (Branden, 1992)

Clayton, Thomas et al, eds.: *Shakespeare and the Mediterranean* (University of Delaware Press, 2004)

Swift, Jonathan: *Cadenus and Vanessa* (1713)

Barnett, Louise: *Jonathan Swift in the Company of Women* (OUP, 2007)

Johnson, Samuel: *Lives of the Most Eminent English Poets* (1779-81)

Swift, Jonathan: *Journal to Stella,* intro. and notes by George A Aitken (Methuen, 1901)

Swift, Jonathan: *The Works of Jonathan Swift: Epistolary Correspondence,* ed. Sir Walter Scott (Archibald Constable and Co., 1824)

Walpole, Horace: *Letters,* ed. J Wright (Lea and Blanchard, 1842)

Cary, Rev. Henry Francis: *The Poetical Works of Alexander Pope* (Appleton & Co., 1869)

Bond, Richmond P: '-iad: A Progeny of the Dunciad', *Periodical of the Modern Language Association,* Vol. 44, No. 4 (Dec. 1929)

Donald, James: *Chambers' Etymological Dictionary of the English Language* (Chambers, 1867)

Griffith, RH: 'The Dunciad of 1728,' *Mod. Phil.* XIII, 5 (1915)

Hamilton, Walter: *Parodies of the Works of English & American Authors* (Reeves & Turner, 1884)

Richardson, Samuel: *Pamela* (orig. ed. 1740; Oxford World's Classics, 2001)

Beer, Gillian: '*Pamela*: Rethinking *Arcadia*', in *Samuel Richardson: Tercentenary Essays,* ed. MA Doody and P Sabor (CUP, 1989)

Dobson, Austin: *Samuel Richardson* (Macmillan, 1902)

Austen, Jane: *Pride and Prejudice* (orig. ed. 1813; Penguin Classics, 2003)

Austen, Jane: *Persuasion* (orig. ed. 1817; Penguin Classics, 2004)

Chapman, RW, ed.: *Jane Austen's Letters to her Sister Cassandra and Others* (OUP, 1969)

Todd, Janet M: *Jane Austen in Context* (CUP, 2005)

Sperry, Stuart M: *Shelley's Major Verse: The Narrative and Dramatic Poetry* (Harvard University Press, 1988)

Bieri, James: *Percy Bysshe Shelley: A Biography: Exile of Unfulfilled Reknown, 1816-1822* (University of Delaware Press, 2005)

Jackson, James Robert de Jager: *Poetry of the Romantic Period* (Routledge & Kegan Paul, 1980)

Poe, Edgar Allan: 'The Mystery of Marie Rogêt', (orig. ed. 1842; in *Tales of Mystery and Imagination*, Wordsworth Classics, 1992)

Hayes, Kevin J: *The Cambridge Companion to Edgar Allan Poe* (CUP, 2002)

Stashower, Daniel: *The Beautiful Cigar Girl: Mary Rogers, Edgar Allan Poe, and the Invention of Murder* (Dutton, 2006)

Wimsatt, William Kurtz, Jr.: 'Poe and the Mystery of Mary Rogers', *PMLA*, Vol. 56, No. 1 (March 1941)

Hawthorne, Nathaniel: *The House of the Seven Gables* (orig. ed. 1851; Penguin Classics, 1982)

Conforti, Joseph A: *Imagining New England: Explorations of Regional Identity from the Pilgrims to the Mid-Twentieth Century* (UNC Press, 2001)

Lindgren, James Michael: *Preserving Historic New England: Preservation, Progressivism, and the Remaking of Memory* (OUP USA, 1996)

Moore, Margaret B: *The Salem World of Nathaniel Hawthorne* (University of Missouri Press, 2001)

Myerson, Joel, ed.: *Selected Letters of Nathaniel Hawthorne* (Ohio State University Press, 2002)

Stowe, Harriet Beecher: *Uncle Tom's Cabin* (John P Jewett and Company, 1852)

Copeland, David A: *The Antebellum Era: Primary Documents on Events from 1820 to 1860* (Greenwood, 2003)

Moss, Elizabeth: *Domestic Novelists in the Old South: Defenders of Southern Culture* (LSU Press, 1992)

Stowe, Charles Edward, and Stowe, Lyman Beecher: *Harriet Beecher Stowe: The Story of Her Life* (Nisbet, 1911)

Varon, Elizabeth R: *We Mean To Be Counted: White Women & Politics in Antebellum Virginia* (UNC Press, 1998)

Weinstein, Cindy, ed.: *The Cambridge Companion to Harriet Beecher Stowe* (CUP, 2004)

Melville, Herman: *The Confidence-Man: His Masquerade*, ed. S Matterson (orig. ed. 1857; Penguin Classics, 1990)

Hayes, Kevin J, ed.: *The Cambridge Introduction to Herman Melville* (CUP, 2007)

Reynolds, Michael S: 'The Prototype for Melville's

Confidence-Man', *PMLA*, Vol. 86, No. 5 (Oct. 1971)

Talley, Sharon: *Student Companion to Herman Melville* (Greenwood, 2007)

Collins, Wilkie: *The Woman in White* (orig. ed. 1860; Oxford World's Classics, 1996)

Hyder, Clyde K: 'Wilkie Collins and *The Woman in White*,' *Periodical of the Modern Language Association*, 54 (1939)

Peters, Catherine: *The King of Inventors* (Minerva, 1991)

De Maillet, Benoît: *Telliamed, or Conversations between an Indian Philosopher and a French Missionary on the Diminution of the Sea* (orig. ed. 1748; trans. and ed. Albert V Carozzi, University of Illinois Press, 1968)

Butler, Samuel: *Erewhon* (Trubner, 1872)

Rushdie, Salman: *Grimus* (Gollancz, 1975)

Hickam Jr, Homer: *Rocket Boys* (Perfection Learning, 1999)

Heaney, Francis: *Holy Tango of Literature* (Emmis, 2004)

Ellenberger, François: *The History of Geology*, Vol. 2 (Taylor & Francis, 1999)

Jones, Joseph Jay: *The Cradle of Erewhon: Samuel Butler in New Zealand* (Daedalus, 1959)

Kilgore, De Witt Douglas: *Astrofuturism: Science, Race, and Visions of Utopia in Space* (University of Pennsylvania Press, 2003)

Carroll, Lewis: *The Annotated Alice*, ed. Martin Gardner (Penguin, 1970)

Brown, Sally: *The Original Alice* (British Library Publications, 1997)

Cohen, Morton N: *The Letters of Lewis Carroll* (Macmillan, 1979)

Hudson, Derek: *Lewis Carroll* (Constable, 1954)

Gilbert, William Schwenck, and Sullivan, Arthur: *HMS Pinafore* (orig. performed 1879; Dover, 2000)

Ainger, Michael: *Gilbert and Sullivan: A Dual Biography* (OUP, 2002)

Bradley, Ian: *The Complete Annotated Gilbert and Sullivan* (OUP, 2005)

Wren, Gayden: *A Most Ingenious Paradox: The Art of Gilbert and Sullivan* (OUP, 2006)

Stevenson, Robert Louis: *Treasure Island* (orig. ed. 1883; Penguin, 1999)

Moore, George: *Confessions of a Young Man* (Swan Sonnershein Lowrey & Company, 1886)

Stevenson, Robert Louis: *The Art of Writing and Other Essays* (Chatto and Windus, 1905)

Wilde, Oscar: *The Importance of Being Earnest* (orig. performed 1895; Nick Hern Books, 1995)

Beckson, Karl E, ed.: *Oscar Wilde: The Critical Heritage* (Routledge, 1970)

Craft, Christopher: *Another Kind of Love: Male Homosexual Desire in English Discourse, 1850-1920* (University of California Press, 1994)

Douglas, Lord Alfred Bruce: *Oscar Wilde and Myself* (John Long, 1914)

Mason, Stuart, ed.: *A Collection of Original Manuscripts, Letters & Books of Oscar Wilde* (Dulau, 2009)

Chekhov, Anton: *Selected Works*, vol. 2 (Progress, 1973)
Rayfield, Donald: *Anton Chekhov* (Harper Collins, 1997)
Troyat, Henri: *Chekhov* (Dutton, 1986)

Potter, Beatrix: *The Tale of Peter Rabbit* (Frederick Warne, 1902)
Lane, Margaret: *The Tale of Beatrix Potter* (Frederick Warne, 1968)
Lear, Linda: *Beatrix Potter* (Penguin, 2007)

Barrie, JM: *Peter and Wendy* (Scribner's, 1911)
Birkin, Andrew: *J M Barrie and the Lost Boys* (Yale University Press, 2003)
Elfick, Ian, and Harris, Paul: *TN Foulis: The History and Bibliography of an Edinburgh Publishing House* (Alacrity, 1998)

Sprague de Camp, L: *Lovecraft: A Biography* (New English Library, 1975)

Loos, Anita: *Gentlemen Prefer Blondes* (Liveright, 1925)
Loos, Anita: *A Girl Like I* (Hamish Hamilton, 1966)

Woolf, Virginia: *To the Lighthouse* (orig. ed. 1927; Penguin, 1992)
King, James: *Virginia Woolf* (Hamish Hamilton, 1994)

Stein, Gertrude: *Before the Flowers of Friendship Faded Friendship Faded* (privately printed, 1931)

Dydo, Ulla E: *Gertrude Stein: The Language That Rises: 1923-1934* (Northwestern University Press, 2003)

Stein, Gertrude: *A Stein Reader*, ed. Ulla E Dydo (Northwestern University Press, 1993)

Toklas, Alice B: *What Is Remembered* (Holt Rhinehart, 1963)

Erasmus, Desiderius: *In Praise of Folly* (orig. ed. 1509; Dover, 2003)

Brecht, Bertolt: *Baal / A Man's A Man / The Elephant Calf* (Grove Press, 1964)

Balzac, Honoré de: *The Wild Ass's Skin* (orig. ed. 1831; Penguin Classics, 1977)

Apuleius, Lucius, trans. EJ Kenney: *The Golden Ass: A New Translation* (Penguin Classics, 2004)

Duchamp, Marcel: *Salt Seller*, ed. Michel Sanouillet and Elmer Peterson (OUP, 1973)

Brandon, Ruth: *Surreal Lives: The Surrealists 1917-1945* (Macmillan, 1999)

Hayman, Ronald: *Brecht: A Biography* (1983)

Kuenzli, Rudolf E, and Naumann, Francis M: *Marcel Duchamp: Artist of the Century* (MIT Press, 1987)

Tynan, Kathleen: *The Life of Kenneth Tynan* (1987)

Gibbons, Stella: *Cold Comfort Farm* (introduction by Lynne Truss, Penguin, 2006)

Oliver, Reggie: *Out of the Woodshed: The Life of Stella Gibbons* (Bloomsbury, 1998)

Cain, James M: *Three of a Kind* (Knopf, 1943)

Fitzgerald, F Scott: *My Lost City: Personal Essays, 1920-1940* (CUP, 2005)

Gado, Mark: *Death Row Women: Murder, Justice, and the New York Press* (Greenwood, 2008)

Meyers, Jeffrey, Wilder, Billy, and Chandler, Raymond: *Double Indemnity* (screenplay; University of California Press, 2000)

Naremore, James: *More Than Night: Film Noir in Its Contexts* (University of California Press, 2008)

Orwell, George: *The Road to Wigan Pier* (Victor Gollancz, 1937)

Crick, Bernard: *George Orwell: A Life* (Secker and Warburg, 1980)

Christie, Agatha: *Ten Little Niggers* (orig. ed. 1939; Fontana, 1981)

Sanders, Dennis, and Lovallo, Ken: *The Agatha Christie Companion* (WH Allen, 1985)

Milne, AA: *War with Honour* (Macmillan, 1940)

Thwaite, Ann: *AA Milne* (Faber, 1990)

Wolfe, Thomas: *Look Homeward, Angel* (orig. ed. 1929; Scribner's, 2006)

Wolfe, Thomas: *You Can't Go Home Again* (orig. ed. 1940; Penguin Classics, 1970)

Donald, David Herbert: *Look Homeward: A Life of Thomas Wolfe* (Bloomsbury, 1987)

De Beauvoir, Simone, trans. Yvonne Moyse and Roger Senhouse: *She Came to Stay* (Secker and Warburg, 1949)

Appignanesi, Lisa: *Simone de Beauvoir* (Haus, 2005)

Francis, Claude, and Gontier, Fernande: *Simone de Beauvoir* (Sidgwick and Jackson, 1987)

Williams, Tennessee: *The Glass Menagerie* (Random House, 1945)

Williams, Tennessee: *The Rose Tattoo* (New Directions, 1950)

Devlin, Albert J, ed.: *Conversations with Tennessee Williams* (University Press of Mississippi, 1986)

Spoto, Donald: *The Kindness of Strangers* (Bodley Head, 1985)

Mackenzie, Compton: *Whisky Galore* (Chatto and Windus, 1947)

Hutchinson, Roger: *Polly: The True Story Behind* Whisky Galore (Mainstream, 1990)

Searle, Ronald: *Hurrah for St Trinian's* (Macdonald, 1948)

Webb, Kaye: *The St Trinian's Story* (Penguin, 1959)

Wodehouse, PG: *Performing Flea* (Herbert Jenkins, 1953)

Donaldson, Frances: *PG Wodehouse* (Futura, 1982)

Usborne, Richard: *Wodehouse at Work to the End* (Penguin, 1976)

Pinter, Harold: *Plays: One* (Methuen, 1976)

Billington, Michael: *Harold Pinter* (1996)

Esslin, Martin: *The Peopled Wound: The Work of Harold Pinter* (1970)

Fleming, Ian: *Goldfinger* (Jonathan Cape, 1959)
Gasiorek, Andrzej: *JG Ballard* (Manchester University Press, 2005)
Warburton, Nigel: *Ernö Goldfinger, The Life of an Architect* (Routledge, 2004)

Perec, Georges: *La Disparition* (Gallimard, 1969)
Bök, Christian: *Eunoia* (Coach House, 2001)
Litt, Toby: *Adventures in Capitalism* (Secker & Warburg, 1996)
Chace, Howard L: *Anguish Languish* (Prentice Hall, 1956)
Nufer, Doug: *Never Again* (Four Walls Eight Windows, 2004)
Seuss, Dr: *Green Eggs and Ham* (Random House, 1960)
Benabou, Marcel, trans David Kornacker: *Why I Have Not Written Any of My Books* (University of Nebraska Press, 1996)
Nel, Philip: *Doctor Seuss* (2004)
Schwartz, Paul: *Georges Perec: Traces of his Passage* (Summa, 1988)

Burgess, Anthony: *The Worm and the Ring* (Heinemann, 1961)
Biswell, Andrew: *The Real Life of Anthony Burgess* (Picador, 2005)
Burgess, Anthony: *Little Wilson and Big God* (Penguin, 1987)

Burgess, Anthony: 'A Clockwork Orange Resucked' in *A Clockwork Orange* (Norton, 1986)
Wolf, Werner: *The Musicalization of Fiction* (Rodopi, 1999)

Larkin, Philip: *The Whitsun Weddings* (Faber, 1964)
Larkin, Philip: *High Windows* (Faber, 1974)
Motion, Andrew: *Philip Larkin: A Writer's Life* (Faber, 1993)
'The Bicycle-clipped Misanthropist', BBC Radio 4 profile, December 2, 1986 (Transcript and recording at Brynmor Jones Library, Hull University)

Fo, Dario: *Accidental Death of an Anarchist* (A&C Black, 1987)
Behan, Tom: *Dario Fo: Revolutionary Theatre* (Pluto Press, 1999)
Bull, Anna Cento: *Italian Neofascism* (Berghahn, 2007)
Taviano, Stefania: *Staging Dario Fo and Franca Rame: Anglo-American Approaches to Political Theatre* (Ashgate, 2005)

Lawrence, DH: *The First Lady Chatterley* (Heinemann, 1944)
Lawrence, DH: *John Thomas and Lady Jane* (Heinemann, 1972)
Lawrence, DH: *Lady Chatterley's Lover* (Penguin, 1960)
Boulton, James T, and Sagar, Keith, eds.: *The Letters of D H Lawrence* (CUP, 2002)
Ellis, David: *DH Lawrence: Dying Game*, 1922-1930 (CUP, 1998)

Roth, Philip: *The Great American Novel* (Holt, Rinehart and Winston, 1973)

DeForest, John William: 'The Great American Novel', *The Nation*, 9 January 1868: online at http://utc.iath.virginia.edu/articles/n2ar39at.html

Roth, Philip: *Conversations with Philip Roth*, ed. GJ Searles (University Press of Mississippi, 1992)

Anson, Jay: *The Amityville Horror: A True Story* (Prentice Hall, 1977)

Bailey, Dale: *American Nightmares: The Haunted House Formula in American Popular Fiction* (Popular Press, 1999)

Floyd, E Randall: *In the Realm of Ghosts and Hauntings* (Barnes and Noble, 2002)

Nickell, Joe: *The Mystery Chronicles: More Real-Life X-Files* (University Press of Kentucky, 2004)

Burroughs, William: *Blade Runer (a movie)* (Blue Wind, 1999)

Bukatman, Scott: *Blade Runner* (BFI Modern Classics, 1997)

Nourse, Alan: *The Bladerunner* (Ballantine, 1974)

Stoppard, Tom: *Dogg's Hamlet, Cahoot's Macbeth* (Faber, 1980)

Nadel, Ira: *Double Act: The Life of Tom Stoppard* (Methuen, 2002)

Eco, Umberto, trans. William Weaver: *The Name of the Rose*, with Author's Postscript (Harcourt, 1994)

Eco, Umberto: 'The Author and his Interpreters', in
    Interpretation and Overinterpretation (CUP, 1992)
    BBC World Book Club interview with Umberto Eco,
    December 2007, online at http://www.bbc.co.uk/
    worldservice/specials/133_wbc_archive_new/page2.
    shtml
Preble, Henry: *The Source of 'Jerusalem the Golden' Together
    with Other Pieces Attributed to Bernard of Cluny, in English
    Translation* (University Of Chicago Press, 1908)

Amis, Kingsley: *Difficulties with Girls* (Hutchinson, 1988)
Amis, Martin: *Experience* (Jonathan Cape, 2000)
Leader, Zachary: *The Life of Kingsley Amis* (Jonathan Cape,
    2006)

Coupland, Douglas: *Generation X* (St Martin's Press, 1991)
Asthana, Anushka, and Thorpe, Vanessa: 'Whatever
    Happened to the Original Generation X?' *The Observer*,
    Jan 23, 2005
Coupland, Douglas: 'Generation X'd', interview in *Details*
    magazine, June 1995